Approaching Fatherhood

A guide for adoptive dads and others

Paul May

Published by
British Association for Adoption & Fostering
(BAAF)
Skyline House
200 Union Street
London SE1 0LX
www.baaf.org.uk

Charity registration 275689

British Library Cataloguing in Publication Data
A catalogue record for this book is available from the British Library

ISBN 1 903699 65 7

Project management by Shaila Shah, Director of Publications, BAAF
Photograph on cover posed by models by iStockphoto.com
Photographs in the book posed by models
Designed by Andrew Haig & Associates
Typeset by Avon DataSet Ltd, Bidford on Avon, Warwickshire
Printed by Creative Print and Design Ltd

Trade distribution by Turnaround Publisher Services, Unit 3, Olympia Trading Estate, Coburg Road, London N22 6TZ

BAAF Adoption & Fostering is the leading UK-wide membership organisation for all those concerned with adoption, fostering and child care issues.

Contents

Note about the author

Paul May is a freelance writer, business consultant, and adoptive father of two girls. He is originally from Aberdeen but now lives in London. He has degrees from Oxford University and City University, has consulted in business strategy with many leading companies, and written several books on management issues. His children are slowly training him in fatherhood.

Acknowledgements

Many people have generously given their time, experience, expertise and encouragement to this project. I interviewed many men at different stages of the adoption process, from those who were starting their home studies to veteran dads. I have respected the confidentiality of what they told me, and kept their identities out of the text. I hope, however, that their voices have come through, and that I have represented their viewpoints as faithfully as possible. I hope also that the book repays in some small measure the trust, openness and patience all my helpers gave so freely. I send my thanks to them all, and my best wishes to their remarkable families.

From the academic and professional worlds I thank Gordon Finley of Florida International University, who shared his pre-publication research on adoptive fathers in the US, and Steve Farnfield of Reading University for introducing me to the Adult Attachment Interview.

Pat Swanton at Adoption UK gave great early encouragement to this project. Her colleague Karam Radwan enlarged its scope and ensured its relevance by helping me to reach potential interviewees via the organisation's excellent magazine, *Adoption Today*.

Margie Rooke and Jenny Rigby at the Royal Borough of Kingston upon Thames helped enthusiastically in facilitating contacts for the book's research.

Gill Gray at Coram Family and Jenny Priestman at Brighton and Hove City Council kindly brought me up to date on the progress of their respective concurrent planning programmes.

Sheena Macrae kindly shared her article, *A Dash of Dads*, and allowed me to quote a section of it here as an Afterword.

Shaila Shah at BAAF kindly offered to publish the book and she and colleagues read and commented on the original draft. My thanks go to all of them.

Lastly, I thank Sharon Walsh, not just for her help with this book but for her professionalism and dedication throughout her work with us. Sharon is an extraordinary family finder who has become an extraordinarily good friend of this family she helped to find.

This book is dedicated to all our children, and all their fathers.

Paul May
December 2004

Foreword

John Simmonds

Just as this book is going to press, I have had the misfortune of losing my two adopted children. Not quite at the same time – there is six years between them – and not as an act of carelessness. It is just that they have both now passed the age of 18 and I no longer have parental responsibility for them. At least in a legal sense. In every other way I feel a very great sense of parental responsibility although it is increasingly tinged with some relief that they have both made it through to late adolescence and early adulthood. It has therefore been a time of reflection on what has been – past celebrations and achievements as well as anxieties and upsets. Some of these have been adoption related but most have been those that are experienced by many families: Are my children happy? Are they well? Do they have friends? Are they achieving and are they developing?

If truth be told, I have no really clear idea of what adoption is and what it is not. Over such a long time, it weaves itself into the close fabric of family life, it is there but it is a part of something much bigger. But in the end, I am not sure that it matters to be able to sort out what belongs where – I know that I would not have what I have today if it were not for the opportunity of being able to adopt. That is something to celebrate and we do.

But what about writing this as a father and as a man? There is no doubt that adoption looks like a female-related activity. With the job that I do in adoption, it is rare to speak to another man or even see another man in the many meetings or events that I attend. They sometimes emerge as powerful and important figures but they often seem shadowy or missing. For a generation's achievement in moving towards equality and giving a voice to the perspective of women, child care rarely emerges from its gendered assumptions. Yet adoption has tried to keep up with changing times by sometimes actively promoting and sometimes just accepting adoption by single, gay and lesbian, unmarried and divorced carers. Adoption is part of and sometimes even leads society's change agenda but it is still often not clear what dads do other than rough and tumble play and putting together the parts of the latest complex plastic toy.

Paul May's book will make a significant contribution to changing this. Here men and fathers take their place in the adoption story. They emerge as thoughtful, sensitive, exasperated, challenged, courageous, interesting and important people. People with their own perspectives and experiences but working alongside their partners or others to secure what is best for their children. Adopter dads should – must – read this and so should anybody involved with them. And other dads will get something out of this as well. There is nothing shadowy or missing about these dads – they take their place alongside others as powerful, important and unmissable – and that is definitely something to celebrate.

January 2005

John Simmonds is BAAF's Director of Policy, Research and Development

Preface

This book is predominantly about, and aimed at, men in heterosexual relationships who do not typically have birth children in their families prior to adopting. The book also focuses on adoption of children within the UK. The majority of British adoptive fathers fall within this scope.

Having said that, in my research for this book I spoke to men who had adopted internationally, men with birth children as well as adopted children, men with stepchildren and adopted children, men in the United States and single male adopters. I have tried to include nuances learned from these conversations in relevant parts of the book.

I believe the treatment of adoptive fathers presented in this book is generic enough to apply to a wide variety of adoptive situations. I have consciously restricted the huge range of adoptive family situations in order to bring out commonalities amongst adoptive fathers, their attitudes, insights and experiences. I have therefore neglected some major areas of the adoption field, reasoning that other writers have made better treatments of these subjects in other books. For example, there is no specific discussion of adopting disabled children in this book; however, I hope this omission will not affect the usefulness of the book to a dad adopting a child with a disability.

The principal assumptions I have made in the book accord with the majority situation as I found it in the British adoption scene today. Readers who think I may have made too much of infertility in Chapter 3 and elsewhere need to be aware that most prospective adopters today begin their enquiries following unsuccessful fertility treatment. Similarly, I talk of the effect that being in care has on children because "being looked after" is what the majority of children adopted within the UK experience.

Within these restrictions, I have tried to reflect accurately the diversity of adoptive fathers' experience. I therefore look at routes to adoption through different kinds of agency, and at different approaches to matching.

The law and practice of adoption in the UK is currently changing. The proposed changes do much to standardise best practice within the profession, and to support adoptive families. This book does not discuss the legal side of adoption in depth, but it does bring out the most relevant features of the studies and consultations that went into the formation of the new law. My touchstone throughout has been to ask myself whether a particular topic will help a prospective or practising adoptive father to be a better resource to his child, or help his social worker, friends, family or work colleagues to support him in his mission of fatherhood.

I have briefly described the main stages of the adoption process and key terms in the language of adoption so that the content of the book will make sense to those who are thinking about adopting as well as to those who are familiar with it. However, this book does not aim to be an authoritative guide to adopting: those seeking a sound and up-to-date guide will find BAAF's standard work *Adopting a Child* (Lord, 2002) invaluable.

This book is, as far as I know, the first book-length treatment of adoptive fathers that has been written. I may well have got many things wrong, for which I humbly apologise. But if I have helped to create a space in which adoptive fathers and the people around them can create debates, inform each other, and progress our understanding of how fathers can help to make successful placements of children who need dads, then the book will have served its purpose. There is a large proportion of opinion in this book, culled from adoptive fathers and the people who work with them, but I take responsibility for all the content and claim any mistakes and misrepresentations as my own. I welcome criticism, additions, bouquets and brickbats via BAAF.

1

Introduction

www.iStockphoto.com

The mainstream, rose-tinted view of adoptive families can be quickly summed up in two rhetorical questions well-meaning outsiders fire at such families. To the children they say: *Aren't you lucky?* To the mothers they say: *Aren't you brave?* If the father's there, they might also say: *Aren't you supposed to be at work?*

People on the receiving ends of these propositions often wince, smile and change the subject. But occasionally an adopted person will point out there's nothing particularly "lucky" about losing your birth parents. And an adoptive mother might counter that she is no more "brave" than any other mother. Dad's not expected to provide an answer, but to get on with something useful.

Our understanding of fathers, their roles and their purpose is vague at the best of times. Those who become fathers by adopting are seen – when they are noticed at all – as instant dads: beings who have been transformed overnight by a happy accident into fully-equipped, fully-functional, regular-grade fathers. They are part of a fantasy of instant, off-the-shelf families: take some children, a new mum, then just add dad, shake, and stand well back.

The "instant" families created by adoption are long in the making, and are not produced using a simple formula. Artificial they may be, but simple they are not. Amidst the diversity of today's adoptive families, fathers stand as largely silent and unstudied figures. Yet, as key figures in their children's lives, they play a crucial role in the success or failure of adoptive placements. How they motivate themselves, how they manage their parental role and how they interact with those around them may all play a part in whether or not our community's adopted children grow up to live happy, secure and authentic lives.

Adult roles in adoption

The central principle of adoption is the interest of the child. Although prospective adoptive parents inevitably begin to consider adoption as a solution for their own family issues, the processes of assessment, education and matching they subsequently engage in are all primarily geared towards ensuring the welfare, safety and development of children who, through no action of their own, become separated from their birth families.

Although this book is for and about adoptive fathers, I don't mean to challenge adoption's essential focus on the needs and well-being of children. This isn't a book intended to skew the complex picture of adoption, with its many roles, relationships and goals, in favour of adopted fathers. Nor is it a more general attempt to describe the challenges or rewards of adoptive parenthood at the expense of the challenges and losses of birth families.

Adoption is not some straightforward transaction in which children are delivered out of one family situation into a "better" one. But it is a process that can meet children's entitlement to a safe and loving family environment where their best option – their birth family – is unavailable because of abuse, neglect or incapacity.

With the child at the centre of concerns, the other players in adoption make up a surrounding structure, and each has an important and distinct relationship with the child. In years gone by, the adoptive mother was frequently regarded as the most important of the adult figures in this structure. The "tragedy" of childlessness (as it was, and usually still is, seen) on the part of one would-be mother was thought to be balanced by the tragedy of childbirth by some shouldn't-be mother. As contraception and abortion became widely available in this country, and as attitudes to single-parent families softened, the supply of babies "put up" for adoption dwindled. As few as 200 children under one are now adopted in an average year in the UK. The morality, and the arithmetic, of adoption have changed radically during the last generation. It's now impossible to see adoption as a means of satisfying a maternal longing in a childless woman, though the biological imperative of motherhood of course remains a strong motivation to adopt.

In more recent years, the adult focus amongst adoption professionals has shifted to the situation of the birth mother. Many birth mothers whose babies were taken from them under the banners of necessity or propriety in a different moral regime are rightly angry at the losses they suffered. Today's mothers have less to fear from automatic judgements about their suitability or desirability as parents, yet they have legitimate fears about the state's involvement with their families. As we learn more about the cycles of abuse that visit families down the generations, it becomes hard not to regard many, if not all, birth mothers of adopted children as victims themselves: people who might have been saved from lives that turned out badly, had we only intervened at an earlier stage.

Of course, birth mothers and adoptive mothers share an attribute more significant than their sex: the fact that they are adults. Their ability to articulate their needs and views may vary, but that ability will always be greater than that of the children. Strangely enough, the other principal adults involved in the adoption construct – the birth father and adoptive father – are rarely heard from. This is hard to credit when men have successfully colonised every other area of human activity (except feminism, where the entry requirements are anatomically strict). This can't be due to a lack of interest in family matters: men are prominent in the field of reproductive technology, for example. Why are the men on Planet Adoption so invisible?

Birth fathers are beginning to loom larger in discussions about adoption. A growing interest in their role parallels a growing focus on fathers' roles in the wider context of society as a whole. We now agonise about the effects on children of absent fathers. Fathers lost to prison or demanding jobs are now a source of worry to social services and educationalists, while fathers who evade their economic duty are assessed and monitored by the Child Support Agency. Advances in genetic testing allow us to determine paternity in cases where fatherhood is disputed. Men are now being identified much more strongly with the responsibilities of fatherhood. Not surprisingly, the responsibilities and challenges of fatherhood are something that men increasingly agonise about, in print and in the pub.

Fathers and rights

I believe that while attitudes to women in adoption have been governed by ideas about *needs*, attitudes to men are underpinned by concepts of *rights*. Men figure in general discussions about fatherhood in the context of their rights to have children, and their rights to have access to their children. In some places, a concentration on rights leads to conflicts that defy any notion that the child's interests are at the centre of the adults' concerns. These conflicts cast fatherhood as an oppositional, property-claiming position.

Perhaps the most notorious of these situations is in Florida, where the state's "Scarlet Letter" law requires mothers planning to offer their babies for adoption to ensure the child's father has an opportunity to contest the decision. She must, if no longer in contact with the father, advertise her intention and ask him to come forward to give his consent to the adoption plan. In a case where the child is the result of a rape, Florida law seems to require newspapers simultaneously break one law whilst upholding another. By running a woman's legally mandated "Scarlet Letter" ads, a newspaper is breaking its legal responsibility to keep the identity of rape victims private. It is hard to imagine the insult this Florida law adds to the injury of rape, and harder to imagine a similar law being passed in the UK or Europe. The rights of the child seem to have been lost in a conflict based on property.

Although the "Scarlet Letter" law is an extreme example of a rights-based, pro-father stance, the notion of fathers' rights is gaining momentum in the mainstream. Surveys continually point to growing worries about fathers' involvement with their families, and particularly the demands that work makes on fathers. Rights to paternity leave have been pursued vigorously, and the "work/life balance" is regularly cited as a stress point for men. The pressure group, Families Need Fathers, campaigns to ensure fathers have equal opportunities to parent their children, especially following separation and divorce. The more flamboyant Fathers4Justice movement grabs headlines and TV time by dressing up in superhero costumes, scaling tall buildings and, well, standing there.

Although I have not detected any organised movement for adoptive fathers' rights, I do sense the concept of rights permeates the whole spectrum of fatherhood. It begins with the separated father's struggle for access to his birth children, continues through (in the adoption setting) the birth father's struggle for recognition as an interested party, and ends with the prospective male adopter's typical frustration with and criticism of the adoption process. Men seem to approach fatherhood issues from the point of view of justice.

My own, perhaps cynical, guess is that these seemingly noble impulses make up for men's inherent lack of a fundamental engagement with parenthood. The noise we make about our rights may distract us from the knowledge that, biologically at least, we have little in-built interest in bringing up children. Alternatively, for those with a more optimistic view of men's motives and commitments, a passionate interest in rights may act to dampen the sense of loss that is the common factor in all these paternal struggles.

My suspicions about rights-based movements may be completely wrong. Perhaps the language of rights is merely a necessary way of arguing about the complex issues involved in how families are created, broken and modified. After all, we make laws in order to regularise our social interactions and to serve the best interests of the community as a whole. The language of rights belongs to the domain of law and its evolution. Perhaps it is no less of a distraction to the real, day-to-day business of family life than any other legal matter.

The present father

I think I'm on safer, and simpler, ground in identifying the key dilemma of the adoptive father. I call this *Present Father Syndrome*. Like any syndrome, it is a collection of signs rather than an indicator of an infection or a defective gene. It's the opposite of a better-known problem: that of the absent father. I guess that many non-adoptive fathers also experience Present Father Syndrome, but that it causes more problems for adoptive fathers.

Adoptive fathers display, and sometimes suffer from, presenteeism. They turn up in their children's lives, and refuse to go away. They're stubbornly *there* for their children. They provide constancy and continuity. They do everything they can to overturn the stereotype of the unconcerned, unengaged father, who they may imagine as their child's birth father – or as their own father.

In the workplace, presenteeism is used to describe habits of over-attendance at work. By being (or appearing to be) at his desk for long hours, an employee might just persuade his bosses he is committed, productive and too vital to let go in the next round of redundancies. Empty jackets warm the backs of chairs so that passing managers will know the inhabitants are only temporarily divorced from their grindstones.

The adoptive father's presenteeism is less self-interested, but it can be just as neurotic. This isn't a tic, or a habit adoptive fathers fall into. Presenteeism is built into the role of adoptive fatherhood from the very start. It is a requirement – perhaps, in the final analysis, the only requirement – of the adoptive father's role. Adoptive parents elect to make a lifelong commitment to another person, without the benefit of a genetic investment in that person or, in fact, an existing relationship with them. They decide to be present.

Unlike most other parents, adoptive parents do not find themselves on the road to parenthood through a single, irreversible event. Men who make their own babies at home (or in a clinic) cross a life boundary at the moment of conception, a transition that is confirmed nine months later at the moment of delivery. For the adoptive parent, the commitment to parenthood has to be made repeatedly during a long and sometimes arduous process of consideration, discussion, assessment and self-searching. In the case of the adoptive father, none of the questions he is being asked, or being prompted to ask himself, during this process is likely to be "natural".

Women's urge to parent is unquestioned in our society. The preparation and assessment of women for adoption therefore seems to concentrate on the important differences between adoptive parenting and birth parenting. The man's commitment to parenthood is less certain. Men are celebrated and castigated for their seemingly innate ability to disregard their responsibilities. Most men, whether they are parents or not, will admit parenthood is something they can take or leave. Whilst good fathers are aghast at the thought they might lose their much-loved children, they also know that had fate dealt them a different hand, they would have found other ways to use their time, money and passions. It seems harder for women to find a substitute for motherhood, despite the struggle they have mounted to play a more equal part in the world outside the family.

The public emergence of child sexual abuse as a widespread problem has also added suspicion to men's motives in wanting to parent a child, even though child sexual abuse is not exclusively a male pursuit. It is vital these suspicions are raised, so that potential abusers can be weeded out of the adoption process as quickly as possible. Yet the necessary assumption that all prospective adopters, and particularly male adopters, are potential abusers is a challenge to applicants who are already struggling to make sense of modern adoption and its fit with their hopes and fears for the future.

The adoption process presents a daily opportunity for the prospective adopter to withdraw. It's all the harder to recommit on this repeating basis when the rational arguments for parenting are so hard to find. In the end, parenting requires sacrifice, if only of the ego. For a man being put through the rigours of adoption preparation and assessment, the knowledge that no balance sheet will ever confirm his decision can be frightening. Adoption isn't something he can approach with one deep breath and fingers crossed. And once he has adopted, he will be under no illusions as to the seriousness of walking out on his family. He will be that anomalous figure: the self-consciously present father.

Do adoptive fathers matter? The overwhelming majority of adoptions are made to male-female couples. Around one in five adoptions is thought to break down (there is no more accurate statistic). For the sake of the children, we need to manage this number downwards by improving the adopter approval process, making the matching process more effective and supporting adoptive placements more effectively. Men play a substantial role in adoptive parenthood: anything we can learn about their attitudes to adoption, and the ways they deal with adoptive parenthood, will help us to understand how they contribute to the success of adoptive placements.

How this book is organised

The material in this book is organised broadly according to the process adopters go through. The book therefore begins with an account of contemporary adoption, what it is and what it isn't, and how men fit in to the adoption scene. We move on to look at how men consider adoption as a life-path, and how they experience preparation and assessment. We then cover the matching period, when approved adopters wait or search for their children. We then explore how adoptive fathers deal with placement, and the period formerly known by professionals as "post-adoption" but always known by adoptive families as "life". The book finishes with some advice from adoptive fathers for adoptive fathers and those who work with them.

This book seeks to add colour to the adoptive father's somewhat sketchy place in the contemporary map of adoption. It's far from being the last word on the subject. But it is, as far as I know, the first time any attempt has been made to explore adoptive fatherhood as a topic in its own right. The book attempts to place adoptive fathers within a web of relationships so those relationships can be better understood, and supported, by all involved in adoption today – not least the adoptive fathers ourselves.

And I do say "ourselves". As an adoptive father, I am touched by many of the issues explored in this book, and I hope I can empathise with them all. My wife and I adopted two girls, sisters, who came to us in 2001 when they were two and three years old. We have no birth children of our own. I have tried not to make this book about myself or my family, though I doubt I have been completely objective. The more I researched the subject and talked to adopters the more I appreciated the diversity of the adopter population. Yet I was also struck by the regularity with which common themes sang through the variety of detail. It's this commonality I have tried to represent, and which I hope I have detected and reflected faithfully. For any detectable bias, or any error of fact or representation, I apologise.

I have generally designated social workers as "she", since most of them are. I have also used "she" to refer to the adopted child, as slightly more girls are adopted annually than boys, and because – this being a book about men – "he" already gets good coverage.

I occasionally address prospective adoptive dads directly in the text, and I hope readers who are not adoptive fathers will forgive this stylistic oddity. I have used this technique in order to create a contrast with the specialised and somewhat formal jargon of adoption workers. I hope the use of this style will help those who work with adoptive fathers to experience their clients' viewpoints, just as my use of professional terminology is intended to help adopters understand the social worker's viewpoint.

A world of difference

www.iStockphoto.com

There's no such thing as a normal family. You find ways of working round what life throws at you.
Single adoptive father

In this chapter we look at what makes adoptive fathers different from other people, and what makes them similar to each other. We deal with ideas about normality: normal families, normal dads, and normal adoptive dads. We also explore the research that has been conducted into fatherhood and adoptive fathers.

The constructed family

Fatherhood is a much-studied but still poorly understood area of human experience. We will be contrasting non-adoptive fatherhood with adoptive fatherhood throughout the book, but for the time being we can settle on one simplistic distinguishing feature between the two groups: birth fathers react, adoptive fathers *proact*.

The traditional attitudes to being a father clearly aren't going to work in the adoption situation. An adoptive father cannot slide into it, and figure out how to respond to parenthood when it happens. Adoptive families aren't the result of a little red wine, or a little blue line. They result from conscious intention on the part of the adopters, and terrible misfortune on the part of the adoptee.

Adoptive families bring together strangers in a unique and uniquely challenging common enterprise, and are therefore to some extent random in nature. But adoptive families are consciously constructed, in the full sight of the law, and under a spotlight cast by professionals. Adoptive parents cannot have an ad-lib approach to parenting. Even though, like any other parent, an adoptive father will use his instincts in parenting, instincts alone will not be enough for the job.

Adoptive fathers also live with the knowledge that at some stage their children may want to seek, and meet, their birth families. For families with open adoptions, relationships between the adoptive and birth families can continue through regular contact sessions throughout the child's life. For the majority of adoptive families, the birth parents remain virtual family members rather than real ones. Birth mum will be mentioned fairly often, and always positively. But all adopted children have the right to know who their birth parents are, and, preferably with support from an adoption agency, make contact with them at an appropriate time.

The fact that his children may want to contact their birth parents at some point, and his responsibility to keep the birth parents' identity and memory alive for the children, can reinforce the adoptive father's perception that he does not "own" the children. Although all parents surely hope they will continue to enjoy relationships with their children when they are grown up and have flown the nest, adoptive parents know there is a potential challenge to their position as favoured parents.

It may sound as if adoptive parents are sadly burdened by a tragic rivalry that may explode the family they have built. And many adoptive parents do feel challenged at the time their children seek to meet their birth parents. However, their role at this time is often one of support, since the children are rarely seeking to swap one set of parents for another, but are merely trying to complete their understanding of their lives and the significant people in their lives.

We should perhaps feel more concern for any non-adoptive parents who blithely assume their children will owe some kind of automatic loyalty when they are old enough to make their own choices concerning the people with whom they live and maintain contact. The real rivalries for a grown-up child's attention and affection are their potential partners, rarely alternative parents.

The adoption triangle

The adoption triangle is a model traditionally used by adoption workers to help prospective adopters understand their role as parents. The model ensures the birth parents are not excluded from an understanding of the child's origins and connections, and it makes the child an equal player in the web of relationships. The relationships making up the triangle are understood to persist for life, even though the birth parent and adopted child may have no direct contact for many years, or indeed at all, after the child's placement.

Figure 1: The adoption triangle

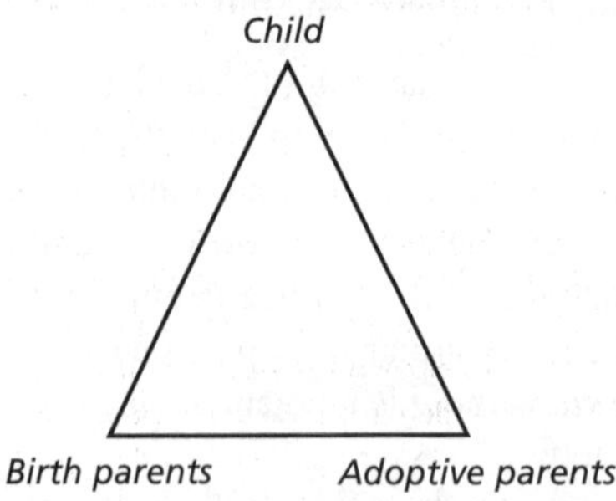

The triangle is perhaps the first structure prospective adopters are given to help negotiate their difference from other parents. It's here they find their new role, and here they learn to respect the richness of the family situation they are contemplating. This is also the point where their vocabulary begins to change as they start to absorb new ideas about how families are created. They will begin to talk of "birth parents" rather than "natural parents" or "real parents" – terms non-adopters use somewhat thoughtlessly. The implication that adoptive parents are "unreal" or "unnatural", second-best or in some way false, is hardly helpful to prospective adopters' sense of purpose.

Adoptive parents rarely talk about their children's birth parents outside of the immediate family. This may create the impression that adoptive parents suppress the existence of their children's birth parents, when it is more likely they choose this behaviour out of respect for the child's privacy. The birth parents are likely to be well-known, if absent, figures within the family, since these days adoptive families do not shield their children from knowledge of their adoptive status. In fact, adoptive parents generally ensure they present positive accounts of birth parents to their children, knowing this will help with their self-esteem, and also mindful of the adopted child's right to know of and seek out her birth parents.

The idea of the "triangle" figure is that the three sets of people are

Open adoption

An open adoption is one in which the three points of the adoption triangle remain in constant contact. The child's contact with her birth parent(s) may be formalised and regular, or organised on a much more fluid basis. Open adoption is relatively new, so there is little information on its impact on adopted children. In any case, the wide variations in open adoption arrangements may mean there are few points of useful comparison amongst the different families. Discussing open adoption in his book, *Adoption: The Life Long Search for Self*, psychologist David Brodzinsky (1993) summarises the main pros and cons for open adoption, from the point of view of the child's benefits. On the positive side, open adoptions remove the possibility of the child's fantasising about her origins, and make her birth mother a recognised member of the extended family. The child can ask her birth mother for details about her background or her relatives, thus filling in the picture of her life from the best possible source. On the negative side, open adoption can introduce ambiguity into the child's understanding of who she is and where she belongs. The arrangement may also carry a sense of anxiety about the adult parties' ability to support the adoption over time. And if the arrangement does break down, then the removal of the birth parent from the child's life represents a renewed loss – with added betrayal.

Open adoption remains a controversial subject and it is worth remembering that no open adoption is entered into lightly. Relationships that have involved patterns of abuse are highly unlikely to be candidates for open adoption.

interrelated and interdependent on each other. However, adoption workers have begun to believe the triangle implies a tension amongst the people who make up "the corners". Some workers are now beginning to use the friendlier concept of the adoption circle. A circle avoids anybody getting into a corner while providing space for other interested people, including birth grandparents, adoptive grandparents, foster carers and siblings to enter it.

Normal families?

The act of discussing adoptive families suggests these families are not "normal". This is true. But non-adoptive families are neither "normal" nor homogenous. Adoption researcher Gordon Finley (1999a) of Florida International University notes that families come about in many different ways, and that "the best interests of the child" – which our legal and social work systems are designed to protect – are perhaps better defined "in psychological rather than biological terms":

> **Perhaps too it is time for the twin stigmata of infertility and adoption to become destigmatized and to recede from public and private consciousness. Were these "perhapses" to come to pass, perhaps we would be in a better position to determine whether children of adoptive families are in any way substantially different from children of a multitude of other family forms such as intact/biological, divorced, widowed, never-married, single, step, blended, teen, deferred, gay, lesbian, dual-career, military, abusive, HIV-positive, and so on [...] Children of any family form, under a microscope, are bound to show flaws.**

In fact, the modern, default use of "family" to refer exclusively to parents and children with biological bonds is quite recent. The Latin *familia* means "household", and the first definition given for family in the Concise Oxford Dictionary is "members of a household, parents, children, servants, etc". The word's second sense, of parents, children and other relatives connected by blood but not necessarily living together, confirms its origins as a means of defining property rights rather than biological relationships.

"Families" have, it seems, been built from, or coalesced around, groups of related and non-related people for quite some time, and the organising principle has owed more to shared interest than selfish genes. The notion of the family as a cosy, domestic unit "blessed" with children may simply be a romantic fantasy of comfort and control – one that was particularly important in the Victorian era, as parents looked for spiritual reassurance in the face of high infant mortality.

The "nuclear" solidity of the standard family is also a relatively recent invention. People who research their family trees quickly reach an illegitimate forebear in one or more of the strands. The initial shock gives way to an understanding that illegitimacy did not carry great stigma for most people prior to the 19th century. Legitimacy is, again, a matter of property. Rightful inheritance was a burning issue for princes in Shakespeare, but of less concern to ordinary people who had no possessions, let alone a country pile, to pass on. As more and more people moved into the "respectable" classes with the spread of industrialisation and the growth of cities, legitimacy and new standards of moral conformity became the concerns of larger numbers, but not before those same upheavals tore families apart and exposed them to new risks, diseases and pastimes.

Perhaps the fragility of the stigma around illegitimacy is proven in the speed with which birth outside of marriage has become accepted in the UK. The 2001 Census for England and Wales found that 'nearly one in four [dependent children] (22.9 per cent or 2,672,000 dependent children) live in lone-parent families – 91.2 per cent of which are headed by the mother'.[1] More importantly, single-parent families of all kinds have lost the power to provoke controversy as economic conditions have changed to allow them to thrive. Money may not be the root of all evil, but it often works as a short-cut to the origins of most snobberies.

If there's no such thing as a "normal family", it's also worth considering that not all families are happy families. Childless

[1] Office of National Statistics, 7 May 2003; http://www.statistics.gov.uk/cci/nugget.asp?id=348

couples readily lapse into assuming every aspect of parenting is enjoyable, and that any complaining or backsliding by parents of their acquaintance is some kind of gentle sham. Birth mothers often say they weren't fully warned of the pain of childbirth and the difficulties of motherhood, though many admit they wouldn't have listened to any warnings anyway. Childless people encounter, or maybe construct, the same apparent conspiracy.

No parent's experience of parenthood is uniformly joyous. The first sentence of Tolstoy's *Anna Karenina* has resonance here: 'All happy families resemble one another, but each unhappy family is unhappy in its own way.' When we examine real families, we always find shades of grey rather than simple black-and-white renderings.

Adoptive families are therefore normal to the extent they are real families: messy, human and changeable.

Research and the lagging dad

Very little research has been carried out on adoptive fathers. One reason for this is that any research on adoptive placements naturally focuses on the family as the unit of study, and the adopted child as the priority within the family. Adoptive parents are usually treated as a couple, with the mother tending to dominate the focus of the research. This approach is understandable, given the goals of adoption workers (to understand and support adoptive placements) and the typically central role of the mother. But it does mean that information about adoptive fathers is scanty and often anecdotal in nature.

Research that does touch on adoptive fathers suggests there are important differences between the ways in which men and women approach adoption. For example, Marianne Berry (date unknown) refers to research by N.F. Belbas into adoptive parents' attitudes to open adoption, noting that adoptive fathers are 'more hesitant about openness'. This would seem to agree with the intuitive sense that adoptive fathers are generally more hesitant about adoption issues than their female partners, excepting perhaps those men whose motivations are underpinned by religious or political convictions. But this line of thinking quickly becomes speculative. Not enough adoptive fathers have been asked enough well-designed questions.

I interviewed as many adoptive dads as I could find to talk to me for this book, and although their candour, constructiveness and humour have driven the book's content, I'm aware that as a self-selecting group, my interviewees may have skewed the book in relation to the broader views or experiences of adoptive dads.

On the other hand, we have to be clear that adoptive parents are, as a group, a prime example of self-selection. Yes, adopters are assessed and screened and trained and supported, but they enter the adoption process – and embrace it – through their own determination. This is one of the many paradoxes of adoption: an essentially random set of circumstances affecting all the players in the "circle" produces, in the case of the adopters, a highly willed outcome.

It's hard for a layman not to see the sit-com husband, several paces behind the more enlightened wife, in findings such as these from Cornell University:[2]

- Adoptive mothers were more in favour of opening adoption records than fathers: 83 percent of adoptive mothers and 73 percent of adoptive fathers felt that adult adoptees should be able to obtain a copy of their birth certificates; only 9 percent of adoptive mothers and 11 percent of adoptive fathers felt they should not have access.
- 78 percent of adoptive mothers and 66 percent of adoptive fathers felt that all adult adoptees should have the right to obtain an original birth certificate, regardless of when they were adopted.

Rosemary Avery (1997) surveyed 1,274 adoptive parents in 743 adoptive homes in New York State in 1996. US laws on access to

[2] Press Release: "Adoptive parents are overwhelmingly in favor of opening sealed adoption records, Cornell study finds"; http://www.news.cornell.edu/releases/Jan97/adoptionrecord.ssl.html

birth records differ from state to state, with most insisting seekers have "good cause" for learning anything other than their birth parents' names – curiosity isn't enough. This is another surprising difference between adoption practice in the US and the UK, where openness in adoption is enshrined in law. Yet the image of the "hesitant" adoptive dad seems to cross the Atlantic with little interference.

Gordon Finley (1999b) asked a sample of adoptive fathers for their views on adoption, using an anonymous questionnaire that solicited freeform contributions. The main quantitative finding was that while adoptive fathers were overwhelmingly positive about adoptive fatherhood, their attitude to the adoption process itself was negative. While we have to remember these findings relate to men in the USA, the five most frequent reasons given for negative evaluations of the adoption process were:

- tough emotionally / emotional rollercoaster / stressful;
- high cost;
- long wait;
- failed adoptions;
- anxiety before finalisation.

With the exception of "high cost", these opinions fit closely with what I heard from British adoptive fathers during my research. (US adopters may pay fees to attorneys and birth mothers, while the only costs British adopters are likely to face are assessment fees to their [independent] agency for adoptions from overseas, travel expenses during matching and possibly loss of earnings during introductions and early placement.) It seems adoptive fathers appreciate both the difficulty of the adoption journey, and its great value:

> **Strikingly, the view from the bridge of recent adoptive fatherhood was most aptly summarised by one very perceptive respondent: 'Becoming an adoptive father was tough. In other words, the journey has been very tough emotionally**

> **but the destination of Adoptive Fatherhood is great.'**
> Finley, 1999b

Attitudes shared by adoptive fathers

Anecdotal evidence suggests there are three main attitudes shared by adoptive fathers. These are not indicators that prospective adopters will be or should be approved by assessors, but common features adoptive fathers seem to share. These may be inherent traits awakened by the experience of adopting, or habits of thought acquired as an adaptive response to adoption. All of them sit well to the fore of rational attitudes to parenthood, and indeed life.

First, adoptive fathers declare and demonstrate their belief in the power of nurture. They believe they can "make a difference". Many discount their social workers' insistence on the irreversible effect on children of early trauma, seeing this as a personal taunt to their abilities as shapers of human destiny. Others have a more balanced view of what they can achieve through their influence, seeking to ensure their children develop to the best of their abilities in a safe and supportive environment.

An interest in the power of nurture indicates that adoptive fathers are constructive people, interested in the potential for change but not necessarily fixated on seeing family life as a formal project. The mysterious connections between the environment and a person's development can appeal to the interest in experimentation many men have. They can see one aspect of fatherhood as the responsibility to change the variables in the child's environment and gauge the effect. This outlook has the virtue of reminding adoptive fathers they are themselves an important variable in the family environment, and may serve to transmute otherwise crippling self-consciousness into useful self-awareness.

Second, adoptive fathers seem to reach a sense of reconciliation with the limits of our personal power over events or circumstances. This is clearly wisdom we all need to acquire, but which men may ordinarily be able to defer for lengthy periods, and sometimes for life. Brought up to compete and create, most men inhabit a world where progress is measured and rewarded. Applying the same values and strategies to family life is likely to produce anxious and rebellious children, even where the force of the father's will produces the semblance of compliance. But adoptive fathers build their families on a compromised foundation. Adoptive families emerge from a combination of random, unfair and often depressing circumstances and adoptive fathers are therefore unlikely to believe life does, or should, run smoothly.

Last, adoptive fathers tend to communicate a holistic appreciation of the characters, needs and achievements of children. They are more likely to present a structured and rounded description of what a happy child is than dismiss the question or snatch at a simple image. They have clearly thought hard about who their children are, and why their lives have become tied to their own.

However, adoptive dads – like anyone else – do not consistently act according to their beliefs. It's easier to maintain balanced and reasonable attitudes to the task of child-rearing when the child in question is not throwing a tantrum at your feet. It may be that adoptive fathers are eloquent in their beliefs about nurture, power and holism because they need constantly to reaffirm those values as a bulwark against residual feelings of alienation from their children. Although time is the great healer, even adoptive fathers of many years' standing can experience occasional feelings of distance from their children and they may need to hear themselves reassert their beliefs to reassure themselves about their commitment.

It's easy to make a list of what adopters are not. On the whole, adoptive dads are not selfless, fearless, indestructible or visionary. They are neither martyrs, nor holy fools. These observations apply to women too, but the ordinariness of adopters is perhaps easier to remark amongst men. Since men supposedly have no "natural" affinity with parenting, nor any robust reputation for taking parenting seriously, we might expect adoptive fathers to display super-human powers of love, tolerance and guidance. But while their take on parenting may be more self-conscious than that of non-adoptive fathers, their awareness does not necessarily make their approach to the task of parenthood any more obviously noble or heroic.

While they universally characterise the adoption process as "an emotional rollercoaster", adoptive fathers use gentler imagery to describe the ups and downs of family life as it develops over the years. Many of them come to decide (or rediscover) that the uncertainty of life can be fun rather than frightening; that life is, in many respects, a game. Several adoptive dads told me their chief reward as parents was simply in seeing 'how things turn out'. If adoptive families have anything to teach other families it is their living demonstration that though none of us has complete control over our lives, our actions need not be futile.

The new new man

Adoptive fathers tend to recognise quickly that parenting involves a huge number of issues that are completely unconnected to the birth process, and that the roles of the father (in every type of family) have been given very little attention. While "mothering" has many meanings in our language (including the idea of being over-protective towards another person), "fathering" only refers to the contribution of sperm. While "mothering" can go on for years, "fathering" is over in an instant. This picture is of little help to the Present Father. A father with both birth and adopted children told me:

> **There is no magic "x" ingredient that turns you into a parent just because you conceived a child.**

Even when fathers have had their ongoing role beyond conception recognised, they have traditionally been seen as remote figures. It is relatively recent that fathering (in the sense of being-a-Present-

Father) has become a topic of concern. Discussion of fathers' roles remains stuck at various pinch-points, including the payment of maintenance by absent fathers and the lack of good role models for boys. Prospective adopters are introduced to the idea of "good enough parenting", an approach to parenting that stresses practical techniques, perspective and calmness. I suspect many prospective adopters also consciously or unwittingly grasp a further meaning of "good enough": that they do not have to be perfect to be approved as adopters.

The advice to remember that your parenting can be "good enough" is under constant siege in the media. Men are unused to having unwanted advice about their personal performance thrown at them, and seem less tolerant than women of the detailed (and often contradictory) parenting advice that floods the bookstores and leaks into the features sections of our daily papers. Parenting is frequently judged in the media, with celebrity parents bearing the brunt of the attention. Even parenting materials aimed at men come wrapped in safe masculine references: the cover of the first issue of *Dad* magazine (2003) promised 'David Beckham on why fatherhood is more important than football' and 'Pierce Brosnan: James Bond's tips for fatherhood'.

In a wide-ranging study of the meanings and experiences of fatherhood, Adrienne Burgess (1997) examines the gulf between images of fatherhood and actual practice. She finds stereotypes of fatherhood down the ages both distract from how fathers actually operate and influence how they may think they should act. Myths, published advice to fathers, and influential (though often faulty) early studies of families have created a body of imagery that doesn't necessarily overlap with real life, but which may nevertheless exert pressures on men. It seems real fathers behave in a multiplicity of ways, and that neither averages nor outstanding examples act as any sure guide to how a man approaches his role as a parent.

Burgess (1997) also points out that memory of how we were parented affects the way we assess our own parenting. For example,

> **The belief that fathers are more involved than their own fathers has been around for several generations. Certainly, most contemporary adults do not remember their fathers as being involved in infant care. However, a study of parents in Nottingham in the 1960s showed that even at that time one in five fathers regularly changed their babies' nappies, one in three frequently put them to bed and one in two got up to them, at least occasionally, in the night. This would have been remembered by few of their children, and it may well be that even today's nappy-changing "new dads" will be remembered as uninvolved by many of their offspring.** (p70)

But the sheer variation amongst families means that even without the blurring effects of memory it is hard to be certain about men's parenting. Research published by the Equal Opportunities Commission (2003) found that British fathers undertake one third of all childcare – and would do more if they had more flexible working arrangements. This finding was greeted with incredulity when it was announced, as was the report's comment that fathers of children under five had raised their daily level of "child-related activities" from less than 15 minutes in the mid-1970s to two hours. Perhaps more convincing than the surveyed childcare hours is the report's articulation of fathers' commitment to "being there". One father describes his role as:

> **Being available when they need it, being a good role model, being their mate, empathising with them, facilitating them to develop and learn . . . Being around and being part of their lives really.**

Their anxiety to be Present Fathers may well combine with a natural tendency to misjudge time to inflate men's reported involvement with their children. Burgess (1997) notes a study from 1971 that measured fathers' interactions with their infant children. While the fathers guessed they were spending 15 or 20 minutes per day interacting vocally with their babies, they were in fact putting in an average of only 37.7 seconds.

What about "quality time" – the idea that short periods spent interacting can be as valuable as long ones, as long as they are invested with richness? Quality time is another slippery concept that means different things to different people:

> **The man whose lunatic working hours prohibit him from seeing his children awake from Monday to Friday – unless, of course he and his partner wish to be relieved of their house – may compensate richly for this absence at weekends, while the daily involvement of the sort of father who is always on hand to entertain his brood by showing them how a tomato will explode in a microwave then leaves mum to clear up the mess is not quite being the male role model most of us would applaud. Unvarnished paternal puerility at large in the home is just the thin end of a wedge which thickens damagingly towards outright domestic idleness and worse.**
> Hill, 2003

Dave Hill, who created this marvellous image, told me separately that we have to recognise that not all working dads fall into the Weekend Dad trap:

> **Many fathers have limited time to spend with their children due to long working hours over which they have no control. In such circumstances weekends and**

> **holidays may be all they have, and some do extremely well in those difficult circumstances.**

Burgess identifies "the playful father" as a leading stereotype that emerged in the early 20th century, and suggests that it fits well with the reality of the working father, turning up late in the day but acting as high-octane light relief.

If working fathers have problems acquiring authenticity in their roles, adoptive fathers must also deal with the burden of the committed, legalised presence they fought for during the adoption process. But the self-consciousness of the adoptive father can obstruct the development of his relationships with his children. The effects of parental anxiety are well known in many settings, and it is perhaps ironic that much self-consciousness is generated by well-meaning advice manuals:

> **When emotions are not out of control, parents can be patient, but there do come times when emotions get the better of patience. When, on the other hand, we try to be patient because we have been advised to be so, regardless of our feelings, it does not come naturally, and then we are pretending with our children.**
> Bettelheim, 1987 (p30)

Though they are usually loath to say so, adoptive fathers generally show signs they are aware of the *pretence* that so often is the flipside of *presence*. American voices on adoption are often more robustly accepting of the occasional and unpredictable artificiality of adoptive family life: one widely quoted maxim for adoptive parents worried about whether or not they can learn to love their newly adopted child is to "fake it till you make it". While this may shock those with a romantic ideal of family life, it is a strategy deployed universally by parents of all kinds at some time or another.

Adoptive fathers seem to feel the need to qualify the feelings of frustration and anger they sometimes have towards their children, ever mindful that someone, somewhere is ready with the riposte 'well, you chose to have them'. They are particularly wary of voicing their feelings of alienation from their children, perhaps unaware all parents have the same experiences. In fact, birth fathers may be more disconcerted by their occasional feelings of detachment from their children since their emotions contradict their evident genetic relationship. But while birth fathers are likely to shake their heads at the oddness of human relationships, and move on, adoptive fathers may become stuck in feelings of guilt or inadequacy. Mastery of the parental role requires them to reconcile themselves to their heightened sense of self-awareness, and to find a way of relaxing into their role that does not deny its artificiality nor undermine its specialness. "The new new man" is not just in touch with his nurturing side: he also knows that the task of integrating a complex set of emotions and values and directing them towards the creation of a happy home is a challenge that must be faced anew each day.

> **You're on a life path you never envisaged. It's okay to be fearful, whatever . . . Just remember that all parents feel like that sometimes.**
> Adoptive and birth father

3

Adoption Man(ual)

www.johnbirdsall.co.uk

> **I read everything I could. Most of it is from the woman's point of view, there's very little about fathers . . . Not much for the blokes.**
> Adoptive father

Adoption has changed a great deal over the years, and particularly during the last quarter of a century. Those who aren't professionally involved with adoption or connected with adoptive families are likely to have fuzzy notions of adoption. Men's knowledge of adoption is usually patchy.

This faulty picture isn't helped by the stories typically presented in the media. Stories about adoption are usually corralled into sections of the media supposedly directed at women – particularly glossy magazines and soap opera plotlines – so many men never come across them. I try in this chapter to give the facts of modern adoption in a straightforward and robust way. My logic is that I'm a man, and I'm partial to manuals. So we'll look at what adoption is for, and address the leading myths about adoption.

We then look at the process of adoption, using the idea of a journey and relating this journey to the formal stages every adopter goes through. We also look briefly at the kinds of children who need adopting.

Finally, we examine a topic key to men's approach to adoption: the fundamental "ownership" relationship between parents and their children, and what this means in the context of men caring for children they did not help to create.

The baby train

For people who are not directly involved with adoption – and that includes the overwhelming majority of people who go on to become adoptive parents – adoption is seen as a service for childless couples. These deprived, inconsolable adults supposedly use adoption as a way of acquiring the baby that fate (and, increasingly, medical technology) has failed to provide them.

This is the first myth to be exploded when someone enquires about adoption. (The other main myths are listed and debunked in the next section.) Adoption is first, foremost and *only* a service for children.

Even those "civilians" who recognise the adoption system is

designed for children and not childless people may seize on the unfortunate idea that some children need "saving". They have an outdated and romantic image of "unwanted babies" being left on vicarage doorsteps, or a more modern and lurid idea of "battered babies" being torn from their teenage mothers' arms in run-down council estates.

There is human drama enough in the realities of adoption, but the mainstream media prefers to stick with a tried and tested formula composed of (adult) misery, bureaucratic folly and unhugged babies. A chief ingredient of this tabloid soup is the idea that Britain's adoption system is designed to *deny* applicants the babies they seek.

A feature in glossy *Real Magazine* (2003) is a case in point. The story is trailed on the front cover as a "Special Report: The Baby Crisis", with a tagline of "The trauma and heartache of our adoption system". The feature itself is called *Wanted: babies*. Morag Preston's article does, in fact, fairly quickly dispense with the idea that adoption is only, or even usually, about finding new families for babies. But she uses the available figures to stress the difficulty of adopting, and to suggest the UK is too bureaucratic in its approach. She writes:

> **According to recent UK statistics, there were 59,700 children in council care last year – 8,944 of whom were under four – yet only 3,600 adoptions took place.**

This makes it sound as if more than 50,000 children were denied adoption in the UK in the year in question. However, most children who are taken into care go back to their own families. Being "in care" (or "looked after", as the current jargon has it) does not mean a child has been removed from her family forever. Looked after children are not necessarily on a transfer track to new families. The casual identification of the care system as an input pipe to the adoption system is highly misleading. Adoption is just one type of plan that may be made for a child, but it is by no means the only one. Adoption is rarely if ever the first plan devised for a child, nor automatically the best plan for any child.

The local authority in my area looks after some 3,000 children during the course of a year, and completes perhaps eight adoptions. Most of the other children return to their families once the reasons for their care orders have been resolved. The authority's eight adoptions mark one kind of success: but the return of hundreds of other children to their own families is as great an achievement, if not more so. Your local social services department isn't stretched because it's busy befouling would-be adopters with paper work. They're trying to heal families.

And, in any case, the number of children adopted from care *increased* by 25 per cent between 1999 and 2002, to 3,400.[1] According to census data, 'since the early 1970s, the number of adoptions in England and Wales has decreased from almost 21,500 in 1971 to just under 6,000 in 2001. However, this was an increase of over 1,600 adoptions (39 per cent) since 1999' (ONS, 2003).

Another way to look at these statistics is to consider that there are around 12 million children in the UK.[2] Around 60,000 of them are in care at any one time. This is 0.5 percent, or one in two hundred. If the adoption volume is rounded to 3,500, then the rate of adoptions from care is around 5.8 percent, or 0.03 percent of the child population; 99.5 per cent of children are not in care, and 99.97 per cent of children are not adopted.

Two reasons given for the decline in adoptions are the introduction of the Abortion Act 1967 and the implementation of the Children Act 1975, which encouraged custody orders rather than adoption for the children of divorced parents. Social factors for the reduction in adoption include 'the increased use of contraception and a change in attitudes to lone parents' (ONS, 2003).

[1] *The Guardian*, 29 March 2003

[2] The 2001 UK Census counted 11,858,857 children between the ages of 0 and 15; http://www.statistics.gov.uk/census2001/profiles/uk.asp

Articles like *Real Magazine*'s piece may press emotional buttons, but they look at adoption from the wrong angle: the external, adult, emotional angle. In the usual approach, such articles see adoption as a way of solving "the misery of childlessness" – of procuring "babies" for "desperate couples". If you see adoption as a service for would-be parents, then it will naturally look over-complicated, patchy and intrusive. It doesn't fit at all well with the kind of customer service we've come to expect from organisations. There's an awful lot of waiting and a lack of guarantees. And the adoption system seems to be distinctly lacking in the happy-ever-after romance of making homes for unwanted tots.

But the statistics about adoption outcomes can also demonstrate adoption is a good route for children. The *Real Magazin*e article says '80 percent of adoptions are successful'. This finding is usually expressed by adoption workers as a *failure* rate of 20 per cent. (The proportion of adoption breakdowns is not known with great accuracy.) If you see adoption as a benefit for grown-ups who want to look after children, then an 80 per cent success rate is an encouraging figure. If, on the other hand, you see adoption as a means of providing a safe and loving family for vulnerable children, then a 20 per cent failure rate is horrifying. It means that members of perhaps the most vulnerable group in our community are being given a one-in-five chance of experiencing another loss, another devastating failure, on top of those they have already suffered.

It's easy to make adoption look like a no-brainer. Prime Minister Tony Blair has taken a personal interest in reforming the adoption system, and drawn attention to the fact that his own father was adopted. Perhaps I'm being cynical, but the combination of telegenic orphan chic – all those photo opportunities with kids in care – and reduced public care bills looks like a recipe any politician would lap up. You don't have to be a genius to spot that every child transferred from care at the expense of the public purse into an adopted family saves the state considerable costs.

We need to be clear on what adoption is *not*. Adoption is not a means of creating families for people who don't have them. Adoption is not a way of undoing the pain of childlessness. Adoption is not an answer to the "problem" of children in care. Adoption is not a way of recycling "unwanted" babies from "gymslip mums" on "sink estates" to better-deserving middle-class parents who have been "tragically denied" their own children. Adoption is not the easy litter of clichés that has built up around it.

But adoption can be a solution for a child who needs a new family within which to grow up safely and happily.

The myths of adoption

There are a number of myths about adoption that sometimes stop potential adopters from ever coming forward. Removing these myths can help people thinking about adoption to focus on the real issues, and to discover whether adoption might be the right route for them. Let's look at the leading myths, and the truth behind each one.

People adopt babies

About 200 babies (children under one) are adopted each year. Your chances of adopting a healthy, "unwanted" baby are very slight, particularly if you are white.

Most children for whom adoption is the plan will have experienced abuse of some kind, whether physical, sexual or emotional, or been neglected. Many adoption workers argue that neglect should be seen as a form of abuse, and it is probably only the accidents of grammar that keep it isolated; perhaps we should simply talk of physical, sexual, emotional and neglectful abuse.

You need to be in a couple to adopt

Single people, married and unmarried couples can all adopt children. An unmarried couple will soon be able to legally adopt a child together (once the Adoption and Children Act 2002 is fully implemented in England and Wales). Social workers may question unmarried couples on their decision not to marry, but only because they need to try and establish the stability of the relationship going forward. But social workers are under no illusion that a marriage certificate guarantees a couple against breakup, so they will be probing the same area when dealing with married couples. An adopting couple can also be of the same sex.

Not all single adopters are women. The number of single male adopters is small but growing. The myth that single men can't (or shouldn't be allowed to) adopt reflects society's widely held belief that men are at worst potential abusers and at best lousy parents.

Only childless people adopt

Families with birth children can and do also adopt. If you already have children then your social worker will work with you to establish what age of child will best fit with your family. The feelings and needs of your birth children will also need to be explored as part of your assessment.

People adopt one child at a time

There are many groups of two, three and more siblings or half-siblings who need to grow up together. The initial work in building the new family may be more challenging, but this is often compensated for by the strength of the existing bonds the children bring into their new situation. Continuity and closeness amongst siblings can be a powerful force in ensuring the happiness and self-esteem of adopted children.

I'm too old to adopt

There is no upper age limit for adopters. You need to be at least 21 years old, but you will not be barred for being over 35, as many people believe. Older parents have much to offer as adopters, especially if they have already parented children. Since many of the children needing to be adopted are of school age and over, older parents may even make a better match than younger ones. And when adoption workers say "older parents", they really mean mid-40s onwards. It's not unusual for couples around age 40 to be matched with toddlers. Where the child to be adopted is 10 or so, the adoptive parents may well be in their mid-50s.

You can't adopt if you're overweight

Not so. Adoption workers are not looking for catwalk models but for ordinary, caring people who can offer a stable, loving home to a vulnerable child and build a lifelong relationship with her. They don't care what you look like. That said, if you are clinically obese and your doctor is worried about your weight's effect on your health, then that might count against your capacity to care for a child.

Adopters must pass a full health check as part of their assessment. Again, the purpose of this is not to establish whether you should be entering the Olympics but to ensure you are going to be available to care for the child for the long term.

Smokers can't adopt

Social workers aren't wild about smoking, but then neither is anyone else. Smoking won't discount you as an adopter, though agencies are increasingly likely to bar smokers from adopting babies and infants under two in order to protect them from the potential effects of passive smoking.

You need a big house to adopt

You need to be able to offer a child a bedroom, but otherwise social workers will not take the size of your house or its rooms into account. They will, however, take a close look at your home to make sure it is a safe and secure environment, and may require you to make some modifications – for example, fitting safety glass in French windows.

We all know house size and location are indicators of wealth and income, so this myth may be another way of saying "You have to be rich to adopt". Class and wealth are not factors in adoption assessment. People of all kinds, shapes and colours are welcomed into the adoption process. Means-tested adoption allowances are available to those on low incomes.

Adopters choose their children, and meet them before deciding whether or not to take them on

Adopters are matched with children for placement with them by social workers acting for the child. Adopters don't decide on who their children will be, though obviously they have to agree to a match and will have had a chance to discuss their preferences. They won't meet their matched child until a placement agreement has been created, which in turn can only happen following approval by an adoption panel at the child's local authority.

Adopters cannot take children "on approval", see whether they like them and then accept or reject them. Children in care who are routed for adoption have already lost their parents, and may have experienced many moves between carers in their young lives. They mustn't be exposed to further potential disappointments, or treated as suspect gifts.

This situation means prospective adopters have to learn as much as they can about their matched child before meeting her. They will certainly see a picture, and may see a home video. They'll also have access to documentation about the child's history – much of which will make for painful reading, and may be out of date. (If your matched child is, say, three years old and her documentation or "Form E" was completed 18 months ago, it will essentially be about a different person.) Some social workers have been known to arrange covert sessions where the prospective adopters can see the child without the child knowing who they are, but other workers do not accept this practice.

People who adopt often get pregnant soon after

The adoption process is not an aphrodisiac. Everyone has heard of someone who knows someone who became pregnant after adopting a child, but it is far from the rule.

Women who do become pregnant early in a placement can face enormous difficulties. Their family situation is already complex, and it can only become more so with a new birth child. They are not likely to reject the adopted child in favour of their birth child, though this is of course a possibility. (Everything's possible.) It is more likely that they will need time and discussion to ensure that every member of the family feels loved and valued.

Adopted children sever all links with their birth families

Although the legal aspect of adoption passes responsibility for a child to the adoptive parents, most adopted children now maintain some kind of contact with their birth families throughout their lives. This is sometimes a form of regular face-to-face contact; more usually, information is exchanged between the child and the birth parents on an annual or biannual basis, using an anonymous "letterbox" service provided by the adoption agency.

Contact with their birth families is seen as constructive for adopted children, giving them a more rounded sense of their identity and helping to dispel any fantasies they may otherwise develop about their origins. Contact arrangements are made with the interests of the child in mind, and contact is never arranged for the sole benefit of a birth parent – or to inconvenience an adoptive parent. Contact may be arranged amongst siblings who have been separated by adoption in order to maintain these important ties.

All adopted children have the legal right to information about their origins.

Adopters are paid by the state

No, they aren't. Adoption allowances are available to adopters, but these are means-tested. Their purpose is to ensure that adoption is socially inclusive and that adopted children's needs are met, rather than to compensate or reward adopters.

That said, even adopters who are unlikely to qualify for means-tested allowances should insist on the continued availability of allowances at the time of placement and ever afterwards. Your child may need expensive one-to-one therapies at some future date, and you never know how your own fortunes might fluctuate. Having an agreement to fund allowances in principle from your child's local authority will give you some security against such eventualities. It's also worth considering that if people don't ask for funding then agencies will not know there is a demand, therefore lowering the pressure for enhanced post-adoption support.

The myth of "adoption pay" probably arises from the allowances paid to foster carers. But foster carers are paid to cover their expenses, not buy villas abroad.

Children in care live in institutions

The grim orphanages of memory have been swept away – or, more likely, converted into upscale apartments. Most children in care – or "looked-after children", as they are officially designated – live with foster carers, some of whom may be relatives or even friends of the family, in regular family homes.

We need more adoption

Not exactly. What we need is a wider variety of adopters with a broader view of the kinds, ages and numbers of children they might adopt. We need adopters who will consider sibling groups, adopters from different ethnic groups and adopters who can offer committed care to children who may be disabled or exhibit profoundly challenging behaviour. In other words, we need to improve the *matching potential* in adoption, so that each child for whom adoption is the plan has a better chance of a successful placement.

The children's charity, NCH, puts it like this:

> **The children may well have already suffered a lot of changes, uncertainty and unhappiness in their lives. The most important thing is that families can offer commitment, flexibility and security. We believe that children need families who can help them grow up feeling good about themselves, with knowledge of their own culture, language and religion. So we are looking for adopters who reflect children's ethnic and cultural backgrounds.**[3]

In an ideal world, there would be no adoption at all. All children would live with their birth parents. Where this was impossible, children would live within the extended family. Our aim should be to support families, rather than pursuing crude adoption targets with no larger context.

The adoption journey

So if adoption is not a simple transaction whereby parentless children are allocated to childless adults, what is it? Adoption is a complex, uncertain and infinitely variable process whereby new families are built around the needs of children who – through, it must be remembered, no fault or seeking of their own – need new parents.

Adoption workers use the idea of the "journey" as a way of organising and explaining the process of adoption. Most adoptive

[3] http://www.nch.org.uk/adoption/showquestion.asp?faq=1&fldAuto=7

fathers take this metaphor to heart and use it to reflect their experiences and explain their approaches to family life. One adoptive father said:

> **It's a journey, there's a lot to think about, and sometimes you need someone to hold your hand. Sometimes you're just scratching your head, trying to think what to do, and you need to talk to someone else who's already been there.**

Why a journey? The principal effect of the metaphor is to replace the idea that adoption is a simple transaction with the subtler idea that it is an ongoing process. Although adoption is studded with meaningful events – such as the approval of the prospective adopters, their matching with a child or children and the legal adoption itself – it's also marked by long periods of waiting, learning, adjusting and adapting. The idea that we are on a journey introduces ideas of origins and destinations, exploration and diversion, achievement and loss.

Journeys are long, often fall into stages, and are frequently subject to delays and changes of direction. All of these characteristics apply to the adoption process. Journeys also involve meetings and partings: we may visit a number of places during a journey, none of which is our true destination.

But journeys are also companionable affairs. We often undertake journeys alongside other people, and meet new people along the way. Adoption is such a process, whereby would-be adopters work with professional specialists, meet other adopters and expand their social connections.

The final destination of the journey differs amongst adopters. However, few regard the moment when their child arrives in their home as the end point – life-changing day as it is. Fewer still regard the making of a legal adoption order as the end of the journey. In fact, most adopters find adoption coincides with their own life journey, and is perhaps therefore a journey without end.

The idea of the journey may strike some men as overly "new age". "Journey" can sound like a weasel word, designed to smooth over the message that adoption is not something would-be parents can transact privately, but a public process managed by an external agency. We can't know for sure, but the complexity, length and public nature of the adoption process may form a factor in some men's rejection of adoption as a life route. But for men who do enter into the world of adoption, the metaphor of the journey provides a useful structure through which to think about adoption issues, manage their reaction to the adoption process, and assess their own commitment to becoming an adoptive parent.

The adoption journey has one very distinctive difference to real-life journeys: it can be cancelled at any time. Adopters have the power to abandon the adoption process at any time up to their commitment to a specific child matched with them for placement. If they decide adoption is not for them, they are instantly plucked from the process, and returned to their starting point. They are not punished or fined; they are not judged.

Stages of the process

The adoption journey encompasses every aspect of an adopter's experience. There is a formal process that unfolds alongside this journey and provides some of its rhythms. In this section we look at the main stages of the process. These stages are described briefly in order to provide reference points for the material in the rest of the book, which is organised according to the process.

Enquiry

Prospective adopters normally begin the process by enquiring about adoption at their local authority's adoption and fostering service, or with a national agency. Many agencies hold regular evening meetings where people thinking about adoption can learn about the process, the kinds of children who need adopting and what agencies look for in adopters. These are good opportunities to ask questions and meet other prospective adopters. Such sessions are also ideal opportunities to hear about individual, real children through (anonymised) case studies.

Would-be adopters may also approach the adoption process by reading BAAF's monthly publication *Be My Parent*,[4] which, like Adoption UK's magazine *Adoption Today*,[5] features children who need adopting. They may see a child or sibling group that strikes a chord with them, and call the contact number to find out more.

Not all local authorities recruit adopters on a continuous basis. They are responsible for supporting the needs of children within their area, and can close their lists when they have enough approved adopters in their pool. However, you can apply to any local authority to join their team of adopters. With some children needing to be adopted outside of their home areas for security reasons, you may be welcomed by a local authority outside your area. Adopters in the south-east in particular can be a useful resource to local authorities in the greater London area or several "stops" around the M25.

National standards for adoption work in England (Department of Health, 2001) specify that enquirers should be responded to within five working days, and a follow-up information meeting arranged within two months.

Information meeting

The aim of the information meeting is to ensure the applicants have heard and absorbed the basic facts about adoption and understand the adoption process in outline before putting themselves forward. If they decide to proceed at this point, then the English national

[4] Available from British Association for Adoption and Fostering (BAAF), 'the leading UK-wide membership organisation for those involved in adoption, fostering and child-care'; www.baaf.org.uk

[5] Available from Adoption UK, 'supporting adoptive families before, during and after adoption'; www.adoptionuk.org.uk

standards specify the agency should provide an approval decision within six months.

Adoption is a bureaucratic process and adopters will become used to writing down their full names and dates of birth many, many times. The first time they do so is via a brief application form that captures their basic details and sets the six-month timeline ticking.

Preparation

Preparation classes form the main part of a prospective adopter's special training for adoption, though the applicant's social worker may set reading or practical tasks as well. With local authority agencies, preparation can happen before, during or after assessment (see below). This is largely a matter of logistics, since preparation classes have to be run for a minimum number of people to make them economic and educationally worthwhile – they include much useful group work. Classes therefore usually include people at all the pre-matching stages of the process, from those who are beginning their assessment to those who have been approved as adopters. Classes run by independent or voluntary agencies are more likely to include cohorts at equivalent stages of their journeys.

Assessment

The assessment is the main business of approval for adoption. It is a lengthy process concerned with two main formal activities: the "home study", and the completion of a report usually known as Form F, after the standard model produced by BAAF.

Assessment should be a two-way process during which the agency learns about the adopters, and the adopters learn about adoption – and themselves.

Assessment is likely to take several months, and the six-month period provided by the national standards is best seen as a reasonable guide to the amount of work required in an assessment rather than a seemingly generous deadline. There is a great deal of information to collect for the report, and little of it is readily to hand. For example, the adoption worker needs to understand the personal history of the adopter, and, where a couple is applying, their history as a family. Few of us have our earliest memories and our immediate family trees appended to our CVs, so generating this material takes time and thought.

The assessment process looks at every aspect of the prospective adopter's family life, the people who make up the family (including friends and neighbours), how the family operates – its style and beliefs – and what the applicant's attitudes to child care are.

The report constructed during this process will also contain an account of the prospective adopters' personal network, detailing the people they can call on to help them in their parenting, as well as the results of health checks and security (CRB) checks, and a financial statement. The health check will be carried out by your GP, who will be paid by the agency for his or her report. The security checks run your name through the police databases for details of any convictions. The financial statement will confirm your sources of income, including any employment.

The social worker will also meet at least two sets of personal referees to gain some external picture of the prospective adopters.

The final report is necessarily a bulky affair, since it describes everything from the applicant's own experiences of being parented to the availability of schools and green spaces in their immediate neighbourhood, plus all the additional external reports.

Panel

The report prepared on the prospective adopter is submitted to an adoption panel run by the agency. Panels are normally held on a regular basis, sometimes monthly. The national standards in England require that adopters be invited to attend and speak at panel, a right that has not been universally available in the past.

The panel itself does not approve the adopters, but makes a recommendation to a decision-maker authorised by the agency. If the panel turns an applicant down, it will explain its reasons. Applicants can appeal if they are turned down, and they can also apply to other agencies without their case being prejudiced.

Adopters who are approved at panel are approved for a certain age-range and number of children. For example, a couple may be approved to adopt one to three children from ages 0 to 7.

Matching

At this stage, children whose plan is adoption are matched with approved adopters. There is no set time during which matching has to be achieved. The national standards for adoption in England specify that no child for whom the plan is adoption should have to wait more than six months to be matched, and that children under six months in age should be matched within three months.

The national Adoption Register,[6] which became fully operational in April 2002, is intended to improve matching between children and approved adopters in England and Wales.

Placement

Once a match has been approved, a plan is drawn up for the adopters to meet the child, get to know her over a short period, and then facilitate her move to the new home. When the child is placed with the adopters, her social worker will visit the adoptive family regularly to assess their progress.

Legalising the adoption

Adoptive parents can apply for legal adoption of a child after a minimum of 13 weeks into the placement. They will of course need the support of the agencies involved. The formality of the granting of the adoption order varies from court to court, but as judges insist on the child being present most courts make the effort to be child-friendly.

[6] www.adoptionregister.org.uk

Adoption support

Most adoptive dads agree that while the preparation, assessment and matching phases are stressful, the real adoption journey doesn't begin until the terminology for the formal process runs out of steam. The term "post-adoption" has been officially withdrawn though it is still often heard. Support after formal adoption has historically been uneven, but the Adoption Support Services (Local Authorities) (England) Regulations 2003,[7] which came into effect in October 2003, should change matters. The Regulations oblige local authorities to supply the following services on a consistent national basis:

- counselling, advice and information
- a modernised system for financial support
- support groups for adoptive families
- assistance with contact arrangements between adopted children and their birth relatives
- therapeutic services for adopted children
- services to ensure the continuance of adoptive relationships
- an adoption support services adviser to help those affected by adoption to access support services
- development of adoption support plans for adoptive families.

With these services enshrined in law, adoptive families will be able to find the support they need without special pleading or falling foul of any "postcode lottery".

Babies, children and human beings

Since most adoptive parents begin the adoption journey with experiences of infertility, it is not surprising that our initial preoccupation is with babies. It's a baby we've been trying to make, and when we despair of making our own, we begin to think about caring for someone else's.

[7] http://www.dfes.gov.uk/adoption/lawandguidance/adoptionsupport.shtml

The availability of healthy, white babies to healthy, white parents is the first illusion to be dissipated in the process of learning about adoption. Of the 5,131 children adopted in England and Wales in 2001, only 216 (117 girls and 99 boys) were under one year old.[8]

> **The proportion of all children adopted in Great Britain who were aged under one decreased from 26 per cent in 1981 to four per cent in 2001. In comparison, the proportion of children adopted who were between the ages of one and four increased during the same period from 20 per cent to 44 per cent. Nearly a third of children adopted in 2001 were aged five to nine and a fifth were aged 10 or over.**[9]

The first statistics produced by the Adoption Register for England and Wales show the massive gulf between adopter expectations – the age ranges for which they are approved – and children's needs.

The graph (Figure 1) shows that adopters are continuing to insist on applying for the youngest age ranges, though it can't tell us how many adopters to the right of the scale started over at the left. Prospective adopters usually start to consider adopting older children as a response to the baby supply problem. As the matching period stretches into a long wait for a scarce healthy baby, some adopters give up. But with luck, and much discussion, many couples arrive at a more positive attitude towards adopting an older child.

In the first place, prospective adopters quickly recognise the baby's fate is to become a child. And children are people, not toys. During the process of learning about adoption and deciding whether it is right for them, adopters develop an appreciation of their

[8] Office of National Statistics; http://www.statistics.gov.uk/statbase/Expodata/Spreadsheets/D6148.xls

[9] Office of National Statistics, *Adoption Orders: Social Trends 33*, January 2003; http://www.statistics.gov.uk/StatBase/ssdataset.asp?vlnk=6381&Pos=2&ColRank=1&Rank=160

Figure 1: Profile of adopters compared to children awaiting adoption. Source: Adoption Register for England and Wales, 2003–4

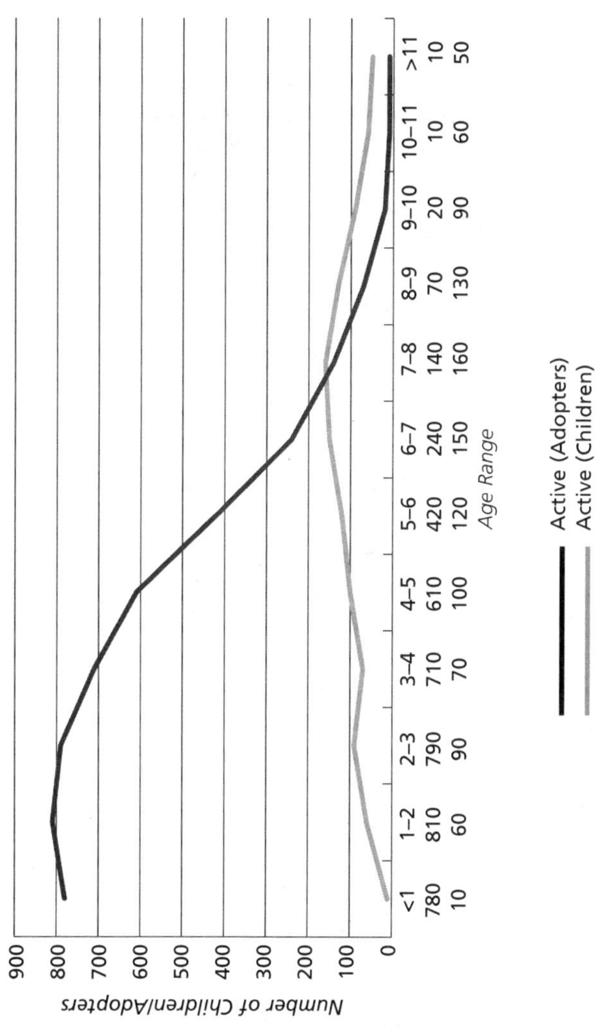

commitment to a human being, rather than a bundle of cuteness.

Adopters are required to commit their lives to their adopted child and act as advocates for her. This means that they need a clear sense of the child's personal rights rather than her decorative quality. The adoptive parent's attitude to the child may sound a little righteous or pompous when presented in this way, but it is only the attitude all parents are encouraged to develop in relation to their child's needs. If, for example, your child needs help with reading or writing, or suffers from an allergy, you would seek out the right kind of help for her, and assert her rights in the school or health system. Parents take up arms on all kinds of issues on behalf of their children. Adoptive parents merely belong to a group where everyone expects to engage in advocacy, and where they share many common issues with other families.

The second step in abandoning the idea of adopting a baby is often that of shifting focus from the baby you couldn't have, to the person you can help. And this person, though they will trail a history that may be unusual and painful, deserves a future as bright and authentic as we, the adults of her community, can make it. We help our children become the people they are meant to be.

Again, this is simply the behaviour of reasonable parents the world over. Wise parents look for signs of their children's interests, and provide outlets and stimuli for them. We frown on parents who force their kids to be championship tennis stars or maths prodigies, suspecting the parents (and usually the father) of playing out their frustrated ambitions through the children.

Whilst adopters are encouraged to consider older children rather than babies, a small number of newborn babies do indeed need adopting every year. These children may have severe health problems, either inherited from their parents or acquired during gestation. Their prognosis may be uncertain, with some likely to have short and challenging lives. The practical skills and personal qualities needed to meet these children's needs are rare.

Prospective adopters are also advised to consider adopting sibling groups of two, three or more children who need new families. These groups are often hard to place because most prospective adopters have little or no child care experience, and feel they can only manage one child. Even those adopters who would like a larger family often assume they will adopt their children in sequence.

However, adopting a second child can often be more problematic than adopting the first, especially if the two do not share any birth parents. The normal feelings of displacement felt by children when siblings appear are multiplied for children who have already lost one family and been asked to accept life with new parents. If birth children commonly want to know "why I wasn't enough", imagine how much harder it can be for an adopted child to accept an adopted sibling. Adoptive families also face re-assessment when they come to adopt again, since the family situation examined prior to the earlier adoption has changed with the adoption itself.

BAAF's Jennifer Cousins (2003) believes the mismatch problem is compounded when children who need new families are reduced to a brief snapshot of special features, a process that tends to highlight their "deficits" and fails to portray the whole child. She is developing a new assessment and linking model that avoids generalised "matching" categories and is led by the needs of a real child.

Ownership and belonging

Our culture lets us entertain two very sloppy ideas about families. The first is the idea that people are entitled to have children. The second is the idea that children belong to their parents.

Most couples who want to have them do indeed have birth children. That's the way we've been designed. But none of us is *entitled* to have children. It's not a legal, or a biological, or a social right. There is no remedy for not-having-children: no one you can sue, no one you can vote out of office.

The majority of people don't bump up against this issue in their lives, just as the majority does not have to face disability or major trauma. But because childlessness is a minority condition, it seems … unfair. Childlessness is not a condition that anyone is trained to expect. It is rarely discussed until it visits some member of a group of friends.

Childlessness also looks increasingly like something science can fix, and which is therefore no longer an issue. Yet, as those who have been through fertility treatment will testify, the "designer baby miracle" is a far from certain outcome:

> **Figures supplied to the HFEA from clinics show that between 1 April 2000 and 31 March 2001, 21.8 per cent of IVF treatment cycles resulted in a birth. For women aged under 38, the success rate per treatment cycle was 25.1 per cent. This compares with success rates [of] 19.5 per cent for all treatment cycles and 22.1 per cent for those involving women under 38 in 1998–1999.**[10]

The underlying statistics[11] show that, for the period in question, 6,309 live births were achieved with 23,737 "patients" treated at 68 clinics. (The breakdown of live births shows that there were 4,621 singletons, 1,579 twins and 109 triplets.)

Reconciling yourself to the fact that no one is entitled to have a child is a tough process. For people who go on to consider adoption, it gets even harder. At some point during the adoption process – when adoption stops being an abstract idea and begins to solidify into a real-life cataclysm that is about to inundate your life – you will have to develop a *new* sense of entitlement. This is the even harder proposition that although no one is entitled to have a

[10] HFEA Press Release, 30 August 2002; http://www.hfea.gov.uk/forMedia/archived/30082002.htm

[11] HFEA, Provisional National Data Statistics, 30 August 2002; http://www.hfea.gov.uk/Downloads/PatientsGuide/PGAggData9901.pdf

child, you are entitled to make a commitment to someone else's child.

If no parent is entitled to have a child, surely every child at least "belongs" to someone? Certainly children need to belong to someone, but this is not a relationship that can only be conferred by birth, or by a court. It's a relationship chosen and defined by the people who invest in it. This is not always clear, because we recognise the dependency of children on their parents. We also recognise that children normally have no choice as to who their parents are. (Adopted children have a dubious claim to superiority here, since those who are old enough to express their preferences can reject the adopters chosen on their behalf.) Yet in the long run families decide on their closeness and the genuineness of that closeness.

Children need to belong; but they are not "belongings". And although children in care become the subject of court proceedings, they are not items to be disposed of amongst more or less deserving adults. We should have learned this simple fact from our wide experience with divorce and its effects on children, but sadly as laypeople we do not always seem to extend our recognition of children's rights from these cases to others.

Many adoptive fathers stress the idea that their children are with them for a fleetingly short time. Although all dads have a tendency to the misty-eyed complaint that "they grow up so fast", adoptive fathers may be more aware of their children's developing autonomy, and therefore less likely to feel rejected when the children start to develop relationships outside the family. Their children arrive with a history shaped by forces outside the adoptive family's control. The family is built through a public, legal process that celebrates its artificiality. It's therefore hard for any adoptive father to fool himself that he has some God-given right of control over his children's actions, preferences or eventual lifestyle. Like any parent, he can do his best to provide a safe and loving environment, and act as a good role model. He may seek to shape and smooth his child, but he cannot for one moment expect her to be a chip off the old block.

Men who reject the idea of ownership with regard to their children as outdated and impractical may still show a natural concern with their children "fitting in". This may be connected to a heightened awareness of genetic relationships and their significance for our identity as individuals and families.

Nature and nurture

Advances in microbiology have made us all familiar with the ideas of genetics and DNA, however hazy we may be on the scientific details. For men approaching adoption, their attitude to the importance of genetic issues can be an important factor in how they think about adoption. How important, for example, is it for a prospective adoptive father that his genes "carry on"? Does he see fatherhood solely as an act of genetic replication? If so, adoption will not look to him like parenthood.

Genetic considerations can get mixed up with beliefs about ownership. If you believe your genes made you what you are, and that the father's job is to make something of his kids, then the absence of the "right" genetic material is going to be a stumbling block in your ability to parent a child in whom you have no genetic stake.

Adoptive fathers therefore tend to be (or to become) strong believers in the power of environment to shape character and life chances. Since men are usually held to be goal-oriented, the belief that they can positively influence the growth and happiness of their children is at the core of adoptive fathers' motivations. However, adoptive fathers are also aware that the genetic inheritance of a child cannot be discounted. One adoptive father told me – not entirely in jest – that being able to ascribe his child's less appealing behaviour to her birth parents' genes was a definite boon. *The Times*'s resident physician, Dr Thomas Stuttaford (2003), can apparently detect the nature/nurture split in adoptive families from quite a distance:

> **Usually a personality trait would not be influenced by a single gene, but by the interaction of several genes. It is interesting that many of the Prime Minister's personality traits can be detected in his genetic father and his genetic grandfather, Jimmy Parsons.**
>
> **However, the character of his father, Leo Blair Sr, was moulded by the couple who adopted him, James and Mary Blair – dominant, proselytising communists. After a left-wing start in life, Leo Blair became an ardent conservative . . .**

In their self-serving moments, adoptive fathers might like to claim their children's good points as products of their benign influence and their less appealing behaviour as inherited curses. In fact, I found very little evidence that adoptive fathers do think in this way; or, at least if they do, they do not consider such thoughts so reasonable as to communicate them outside the family. My impression is that adoptive fathers are intrigued by their children's genetic inheritance, and keen to find out how their heritage will express itself in the context of the adoptive family. So, for example, a child adopted from a family situation marked by abuse down the generations has, in her adoptive family setting, her lineage's first opportunity to discover its talents in a "normal" environment. Who knows what will bloom?

Bruno Bettelheim (1987), while describing the psychoanalytic approach to human development in contrast to the behaviourist approach, echoes the attitudes of many adoptive fathers when he says:

> **The parent must not give in to his desire to try to create the child he would *like* to have, but rather help the child to develop – in his own good time – to the fullest, into what he wishes to be and**

> **can be, in line with his natural endowment and as the consequence of his unique life history.** (p11)

The nuance for an adoptive father reading this quote is the knowledge that his child's "unique life history" falls into at least two major movements: before and after the adoptive placement. An adoptive father tempted to believe that only environmental factors ("nurture") count in child development must still accept that there was a time when he had no control over the child's environment. While there are some aspects of their children they might try to change, there will always be areas adoptive parents cannot reach. Whether these areas are bounded by genetics or early-life experiences cannot usually be determined.

Prospective adoptive fathers' attitudes to the personal malleability of their children are important because they can underlie their motivations for adopting. Believing children's lives cannot be changed for the better will obviously make someone a poor candidate as an adopter. However, believing a child's birth parentage and early history can be disregarded in favour of vigorous, positive parenting is a path that will lead to disappointment. Adoptive families are constructive families, but they are constructed ones too.

> **Once you realise your children are not obliged to like you later on, it destroys any faith you might have in the idea that they are possessions. You're there to help them fly.**
> Adoptive father

Revising the future: How men consider adoption

www.iStockphoto.com

> **You have to be sure in your own mind, committed. It's a long and heart-rending process.**
> Adoptive father

Men's experience of the adoption process is one of alarming emotional intensity, referred to by all the adoptive fathers I spoke to as an "emotional rollercoaster". The calm, organised "journey" of adoption turns out to be a wild ride, terrifying and exhilarating by turns.

One of the key factors in men's consideration of adoption as a potential life-path is how they deal with the issue of infertility. Although not all prospective adopters come to adoption after trying unsuccessfully to have birth children, this is by far the most common background of applicants. And while not all cases of childlessness involve male infertility factors, all childless men considering adoption need to examine their feelings about their inability to become birth fathers.

Fatherhood is a nebulous concept, with no agreed set of responsibilities or approved repertoire of behaviours available to the man who takes it up. Men considering becoming fathers through adoption need to find or build motivations to adopt, whereas birth fathers have the option of reacting to fatherhood as a fait accompli. Every prospective adoptive father must work out his own motivations and satisfy himself – and his assessing social worker – that the motivations he finds have validity and strength. In this chapter we look at how adoptive fathers go about locating and articulating their fatherhood ambitions.

We also look at issues of control and perspective, and how adoptive fathers reconcile themselves to the uncertainty and unknowability of many aspects of adoption.

Adopters' experience of talking and learning about adoption is also covered, as we see how men gather information and support for the life-changing project upon which they are embarking.

All aboard the rollercoaster

"Emotional rollercoaster" is a widely used phrase but is particularly apposite for adoptive fathers. The adoption journey is marked by unpredictable peaks and troughs of activity. This pattern is reflected in the adopter's emotional life, with delays causing gloom and developments causing excitement or disappointment depending on their nature.

Figure 1: The rollercoaster

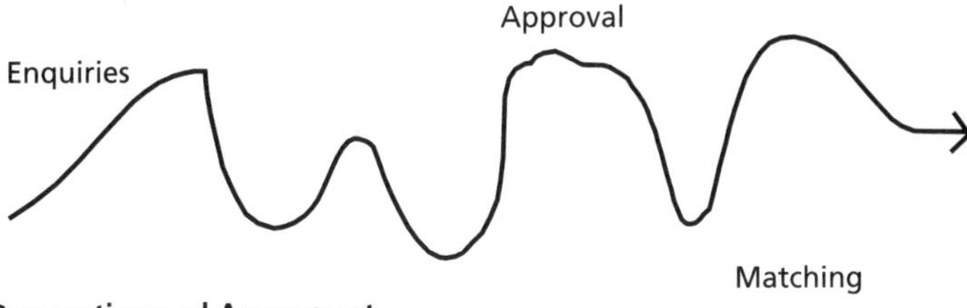

One adoption worker says that managing uncertainty is a major part of dealing with the adoption process. Men may use statistical outcomes as signposts to help them navigate the vague future being blurrily mapped for them, and may as a result become over-deterministic. For example, they may try to find – or demand that a social worker give them – definitive predictive links between pre-birth situations such as maternal drug abuse during pregnancy and future academic attainment of the child. Some prospective adoptive fathers seem desperate for "ballpark figures" to help them shape their nebulous future, and this seems particularly true of the over-educated professional classes. An adoption worker told me:

> **Generally men want to be rational about the process and the pitfalls. That's not to say women don't want to be [rational], but the women tend to be the primary carers, so they are more hands-on. But it's easy for men to get overlooked [in the process] – the women tend to huddle together.**

Adoptive fathers' abilities and preferences are often obscured by the way couples tend to divide up their roles. My impression that men are more interested in weighing up the probabilities of different outcomes is widely evidenced by my research, yet this preference may simply be one element that fills a vacuum created by the female partner's natural appropriation of other issues.

When roles are distributed in unexpected ways, men may be challenged by new tasks – or surprise observers with their competence. This is most obvious in the case of single male adopters, who have to take on all the parental roles, and cannot choose to specialise in some at the expense of others. But other examples of challenges to the default roles of male adopters do occur. Take, for instance, the case where the adoptive parents are to meet the birth father, but not the birth mother. Usually the issue of contact between adoptive and birth families is restricted to the women, since the birth father is absent, unknown or abusive. Men do not therefore usually face the responsibility of maintaining this segment of the adoption circle. Meeting the birth father may threaten the adoptive father's sense of capacity and entitlement. While adoptive mothers can feel similarly threatened by meeting birth mothers, it is much easier for those around them to empathise with the situation. There is no accessible tradition of men undertaking to look after each other's children, making the situation unknown territory for both parties.

Coping with the uncertainty of the waiting period raises insoluble paradoxes for prospective adopters. One approved male adopter who had been waiting a year for a match told me, 'You need to keep your fingers crossed and get on with your life . . . But you can't!' He said he felt his life was "on hold" – a phrase often used by women during fertility treatment.

Judging how much to push their social worker and how much to back off is another source of stress for men at this time. They want to gain some sense of control over the situation, and to contribute to its progress; but at the same time they don't want to alienate the professionals who can bring the wait to an end by finding their child. The approved adopter "on hold" saw himself as potentially in competition with other adopters, if only for his social worker's attention. He did not want to give his social worker any reason to favour another client, but also knew that doing nothing might be interpreted as a lack of commitment.

Adopters with independent agencies are not usually left in this situation. Local authority adopters waiting for a match may be advised by their social workers to take on more of the searching activity, or to rethink their target range. For example, adopters approved to adopt one child aged 0–2 will increase their chances for matching by considering sibling groups or wider age ranges. (If they do change their target ranges, they will need to go back to panel.)

Trouble at the mill: men dealing with infertility

Although they are usually elided in the minds of people who have no contact with either, the worlds of fertility treatment and adoption are light years apart. We have met the main adoption myths; but there are fertility treatment myths too.

Infertility is seen partly as a health issue, and partly as a consumer choice issue. These two views collide in arguments about how IVF treatment should be funded. Even those who are convinced infertility is a genuine health issue acknowledge that IVF is not actually a healthcare procedure. Lord Winston, the IVF pioneer, television educator and Labour peer told *The Guardian*:

> **The trouble with *in vitro* fertilisation is that it's a wonderful money-spinner. It's a brilliant diversion from what's really the matter. It's jolly easy to do, because you can mechanise it. You can just thread people through a programme and you don't need to think. Most women going through IVF are actually effectively going**

> **through a mill. [...] IVF isn't a treatment for infertility. It's a way of getting pregnant on a one-shot basis. It's quite different.**

His candour is all the more remarkable when you know – as Winston did – that the interviewer had just come from her own embryo transfer (Birkett, 2000).

The medicalisation of fertility is one of the greatest complicating factors in prospective adopters' early attitudes to adoption. As long as procedures exist, and new procedures are being introduced, the medical establishment holds out hope to infertile couples.

The causes of infertility are many, and only a few of them have been identified. Fertility experts estimate female factors are implicated in one third of cases, male factors in another third, and joint factors in the remaining third. For every three couples who move from fertility treatment to considering adoption, one will be coming to terms with the female factor, one with the male factor, and one with inconclusiveness. People who intend to adopt have to find some way of absorbing this information, patchy as it is, into their understandings of themselves.

For men, cases where their own infertility is known to be the problem are joined by those where the reasons for the couple's infertility is unknown. In this situation, the man may privately shoulder the blame for the non-appearance of a baby. Where the problem is clearly identified with the woman, the man may feel obscurely guilty for her "deficiency" or for his ill luck in choosing her, or for his earlier belief that infertility would not be a problem in the relationship.

However, the path of adoption also offers childless people a kind of freedom: the right to stop thinking of their infertility as a medical condition. Adoption offers childless couples a means of making families without labelling themselves as people who need medical help.

Adoptive fathers who have been through fertility treatment tend to forget most of the details of the treatment period, though they have strong visceral memories of their partners' suffering – and can usually tell you how much the whole project cost, and how long it went on for. The practicalities of caring for a child and a growing appreciation of the multi-dimensional nature of parenthood, together with an understanding of the special conditions adoption brings to childhood, come as a welcome replacement for anxiety about conception and the feeding of the "mill".

Adoption is an alternative life-path, not an alternative way of acquiring a baby. It's for this reason adoption agencies insist that prospective adopters do not also pursue IVF. In fact, agencies will usually require prospective adopters to leave some time before their abandonment of fertility treatment and their embarkation on the adoption journey. There is no set period for effecting this change of routes, but it is not uncommon for an agency to suggest a year's delay, and a delay of six months tends to be the minimum.

Some men may feel the absolute cut-over between fertility treatment and the adoption path is unfair. Surely they should be allowed to spread their bets? Such men are likely to find the change in perspective necessary for adoption a painful struggle. The pregnancy of their partner has understandably become their goal. But men who ask to take care of other people's children have to see birth as just the start of a much longer and more difficult process: the life's task of parenthood. They must also reorient their thinking towards the needs of those children who, through no fault of their own, and as a result of trauma or abuse, need new parents.

The same shift in perspective can trip men when they learn that, when a child is placed with them, they will be asked to use contraception for at least six months, and possibly longer. Social workers know that asking infertile couples to practise birth control may raise some hollow laughter, but there's no neat or irony-free way of impressing on prospective adopters that the child they adopt has to come first. They should not threaten the security of the child placed with them in any way, including through a pregnancy, however unlikely a pregnancy is to occur.

Infertility can clearly be an issue of self-esteem for men. As several of the accounts in Peter Howarth's (1997) anthology *Fatherhood* testify, one of the early joys of impending fatherhood is the confirmation that 'at least I now know that my guys can swim upstream'. For adoptive dads, there is no such sense of triumph or relief. Being an adoptive parent can seem a mark of biological imperfection. Given the media's casual insistence that "miracle babies" are delivered routinely with production-line efficiency in high-tech clinics throughout the land, the implied sexual dysfunction of a would-be adopter can seem even greater. These people are beyond even the reach of designer-baby science! They must be *really* weird.

All successful childless adopters reach their own accommodation with their infertility. Few parade the details of their medical histories, yet, when asked, most adoptive dads seem happy to establish the reasons for their infertility and then move on. The fact of childlessness has become for them a point of departure.

Adoptive fathers frequently mention the importance of coming to terms with the reasons why they cannot have a birth child before they can become positive about adoption. As the adoption process continues, many adoptive fathers say they move from a position of reconciliation with infertility to an unexpected delight that adoption has become a viable route to having a family. They are surprised at the excitement they begin to feel at the prospect of adopting, and often even begin to see infertility in a positive light.

Their female partners tend to take these developments with a pinch of salt. It's not unusual for men to switch from one absolute position to its reverse, becoming evangelists for the cause they once condemned, before (with luck) settling into a more balanced view. However, I believe that many men hold on to their moment of revelation about the role of fertility in families, and their new perception that families are built through their interactions rather than shared genes. This insight often becomes a key part of the foundations of their parenting.

While the consensus of professional opinion seems to be that infertile couples never completely "get over" their infertility, there is no doubt that adoptive parents succeed in changing their attitudes to infertility. All adoptive parents are vulnerable to feelings of regret about their lack of a blood tie with the children they love, but it is possible to note and accept these feelings without being dismayed or undermined by them. After all, we ask adopted children to accept the fact of their adoption, and to find an accommodation with its special features – and its ambiguities. Why assume an adoptive parent will never be able to reconcile himself to infertility, which – compared to the loss of a parent – is a fairly trivial matter?

But infertility does represent a frustration of expectations. Adoption is a life-path no one envisages: children do not plot their removal from birth parents, birth parents do not set out to lose their children, and adoptive parents have rarely grown up with the ambition to adopt. Some adoptive fathers spoke of their residual anger at their infertility, noting that some element of resentment remains, however small it has become over time.

Coming to terms with infertility requires men to own and experience their feelings, rather than expect those feelings to ever entirely disappear. No matter how strongly an adoptive father feels for his child, there may always be moments of regret for the unlived life. If so, we should acknowledge this rather than seek to condemn or suppress it. The quality of this regret seems similar to that which adopted children may feel, although of far lesser intensity. The adult has lost a dream: but the child has lost a world.

Men coming forward

Most adoption enquiries are initiated by women. Their male partners are usually reticent and sometimes straining to be polite, giving the impression of having been towed to an introductory information meeting. An adoptive father who talks to preparation groups summed up the mood of most men there as "sheer panic". Yet men who become adoptive fathers clearly change their stance, becoming enthusiastic and committed parents, and often evangelists for the adoption process.

Is there a fundamental difference in the way men and women discover and sustain their interest in and commitment to adoption? A woman's interest in adopting is rarely questioned in principle. During assessment and preparation, the prospective adoptive mother will be asked to examine her attitudes to parenting, her feelings about her childlessness, and many other painful but necessary topics. But her desire to be a mother will rarely be questioned. Despite the efforts of feminists to broaden our understanding of women's roles in society, we still take it as read that all women want, at some level, to be mothers.

Men's commitment to fatherhood, on the other hand, is never taken for granted. Do men have deep-rooted, integral desires to be parents? Men who express such feelings can attract suspicions, especially when they dress up as superheroes, scale prominent buildings and hold up the traffic. There's no established tradition of men yearning for children, except in the dynastic sense of men who want heirs for their wealth or titles.

Men are traditionally seen as reluctant fathers, or inadequate fathers, or fathers who adapt to the responsibilities fatherhood brings. These stereotypes all have one thing in common: they all depend on the idea of the man *reacting* to a situation in which he finds himself. Men, it seems, deal with what life hands them; some men cope admirably and honourably, and others fail. But none, in this representation of men, actively seeks the situation of father.

A man's motivation to adopt will be therefore always questioned closely, while a woman's may not. Good practice suggests adoption workers need to question women as closely as men on their motivations, since child abuse is not solely the province of men. But even so, women can call on a motivation we accept is shared by all of their sex, whereas men cannot.

Where the prospective male adopter is part of a mixed-sex couple, disentangling his motivations from those of his partner may be hard for him to accomplish, even with the help of a patient and sensitive social worker. Couples who have been together a long time and possibly worked through the challenges of infertility naturally become protective of each other. Many adoptive fathers who had tried fertility treatment spoke of their sadness at the physical and emotional pain their partners endured, and plainly felt their own worries and frustrations were negligible in comparison. However, if the man's sense of guilt propels him towards adopting as a means of satisfying his partner's desire to be a mother, this impulse will not sustain him through the adoption process and beyond into a successful placement. Noble gestures ultimately make for shaky foundations.

The situation is even harder for the single male adopter. In the first place, few people outside the adoption profession are even aware that single people can adopt children, and many lay people are frankly appalled by the idea of single male adopters. Their reaction usually reveals an idea of adoption that includes swaddled babies being handed out to callers at orphanages, together with a fear of predatory child abusers. An attitude to adoption centred on the needs or wishes of adults will inevitably be unable to cope with the concept of a single male adopter. For people with this attitude, the single man with a child is at best a social disaster, at worst a criminal.

The same narrow thinking inspires resistance towards the idea of gay male couples adopting. A gay couple who went on to have three birth children by surrogacy reported their experiences as potential adopters with a local authority. Turned down at their first panel, they were told they would not be allowed to adopt a "normal" child, but might be approved for a child with special needs. The implied judgement was that as a gay couple they did not "deserve" a mainstream child and should be somehow punished with a more challenging child. The couple themselves pointed out that children with special needs actually require *more* capable parents than other children do – a viewpoint good practice supports but which, in this couple's perception, was not operating at their agency. They attended extra courses on caring for special needs children, returned to panel a year later, and were turned down.[1]

If we abandon our stereotypes and take the child-centred view, then it's easier to see that, amongst the wide variety of needs children have, some will benefit from a strong family attachment with a male provider. Given that many voices in the mainstream bemoan the lack of father figures in the lives of young people, we should be encouraging more men to come forward as adopters, whatever their relationship status.

Finding a reason

Where do men find their motivation for adoption? Since they cannot call on a natural instinct or cite an accepted male drive for parenthood, men have to find and affirm their own, conscious reasons for adopting. They have to construct an account of their future lives that includes children.

Some adoptive fathers told me they found their motivation by identifying specific rewards of family life. In imagining their future, many adoptive fathers envisaged rewards couched in terms of specific desired events, almost like snapshots of the future. Trips to the seaside featured prominently, perhaps hinting that what adopters want most of all is to blend in with the crowd.

When asked to generalise from these images, adoptive fathers tend to identify their interactions with their children as their prime reward. They expect their interactions to be positive, but they also include the more challenging interactions that are indicated for adoptive families. For example, they may look forward obscurely to

[1] *Home Truths*, BBC Radio 4, 2 August 2003; the feature can be heard at http://www.bbc.co.uk/radio4/hometruths/0331gay_dads.shtml

supporting their child in her search for her birth family. This may cause them pain, but also pleasure in their ability to complete their child's understanding of her origins. During his assessment, his social worker will query and challenge the prospective adopter's understanding of the rewards of family life, and ensure he understands the downsides as well.

Prospective adoptive fathers are often hungry for the changes their children will produce in their lives. They crave the meaning family brings to our lives. They have often exhausted the possibilities for meaningful interaction that work and hobbies bring, and long for the authentic experience that living with growing people brings. Of course, some may be disappointed when they find family life is not solely composed of cherishable moments and therefore might benefit from having their expectations lowered in advance of the placement.

Experienced adoptive fathers delight in the perceptions and discoveries of their children. Their children's freshness to the world can be a source of shared wonder in their family as in any other. It's too tempting to see adoption as a situation that permanently colours a family's attitudes, staining any rose-tinted spectacles grey. An over-gloomy outlook can be a hangover from the preparation period, where themes such as the seriousness of abuse and the difficulties of attachment loom large. Without trying to diminish the importance of such topics, we must also cheer loudly for the good things in family life – the good that triumphs over the early evil and misfortune that affect some children's lives. We must not condemn them to lives designed to demonstrate "the classic stages of grief", or "the effects of early trauma", or any other tidy phrase from the literature.

Creating a reason, or set of reasons, for adopting is a tough task. It's one of the reasons the adoption process takes time. If you are a regular guy in a regular couple, your first reason for adopting will most likely be "because my wife wants to". Unfortunately, this reason will not carry you very far through the process. You can't do it for her, or just for her.

As you find your reasons and test them out, you'll also be given repeated opportunities to give them up. If someone realises he cannot be a parent, then his withdrawal from the process can be regarded as a *success* for the adoption process. If a man is going to be a bad parent, then it's better he be no parent, especially when his putative child will already have suffered much damage in her life. But when you are the man riding the adoption rollercoaster, you do not know if you are a future bad parent who should withdraw now, or just an ordinary, scared, underconfident man who is temporarily overwhelmed with the new information he is taking in. These are tough times for anyone.

The pursuit of normality

Men who survive the adoption process intact emerge with solid reasons for adopting. These reasons often evolve during the experience of being a parent. The important thing is successful adoptive dads have reasons *they* understand, which help them through the difficult patches of parenting. At some stage they may be able to echo the reasons of birth parents, who often cite "seeing them sleeping" as all the reason, reward or joy they need from parenting. Until that time arrives – and it may never arrive in quite the same form, or hang around if it does – adoptive dads build intellectual foundations to support their role.

Many adoptive dads mention strong religious or spiritual convictions in their motivations for adopting. However, would-be adopters who believe they are "rescuing" lost souls will usually be asked to buttress their motivations with more down-to-earth reasoning. Some adoptive dads mention political reasons for adopting. Here the emphasis is usually on playing a needed role in the community, rather than changing society from the roots up.

Shifting down the scale of men's reasons for adopting, we get close to a universal motivator for adoptive dads: to be "normal" – whatever that is. Many adoptive dads mention the urge to be like everyone else alongside deeper motivations. At a practical level, even though parents complain bitterly about the child-unfriendliness of the British scene, childless couples especially will quickly tell you how the entire world is designed for families, from the ground up. The calendar revolves around school holidays. If you don't have children, but would like children, you notice the commercial world is designed to service families and singles, but not people like yourself. Of course, if you talk to people who have *chosen* not to have children, you get a different, and more exciting, view of the world. Adoptive parents who yearn for "normality" are choosing one normality among a wide variety of normalities actually on offer.

An adopter's focus on "normal family life" may be artificial, but it is one that is usually encouraged, or at least not discouraged, by the professionals with whom adopters work. After all, "normal family life" is what children who need to be adopted need. The adoption system thrives on people who suspect they are, well, a bit boring. Not too boring, but not *too* exciting either.

Some men pursue adoption through all its ups and downs simply because they always complete whatever project they undertake. These men are perhaps closest to the stereotypical father, putting his shoulder to the tasks he chooses, and never seriously questioning his own commitment. Admirable as they may be, these men are not as thick on the ground as you might expect. The experience of fertility treatment can batter even the most strong-willed man, who may have won all his previous battles in less personal arenas, such as at work. The image of the stubborn male, who does what he has said he will do, come what may, is also out of fashion. We expect our men to be more insightful, more self-questioning.

If there's a common pattern in the development of men's motivations to adopt, it's the passage from reluctant traveller to excited evangelist. Many men do not know much about adoption, and what they do know scares them. The idea of having a *social worker* in the house freaks them out. They may have just poured a small fortune down the drain of a fertility clinic (via a succession of little pots) and feel more like going out and buying a motorbike. The last thing they want is to start on another big family-building project, especially one that's a second-best option for weirdos who can't accept their own childlessness. And when it becomes clear they'll have to go to classes, and have their names run against criminal databases, and learn the miserable and shocking histories of abused children . . . It's a lot to take on; and lots of men say no.

Those who do start on the journey often find themselves being gradually converted to the notion of being an adoptive parent. Like any other formidable undertaking, becoming an adopter has to be approached bit by bit. It's like eating an elephant – an elephant with some very unpalatable parts at that, but one that can be consumed if the portions are small enough, and there's enough time to recover between courses.

There are certain key insights that recur in transforming men from followers to flag-wavers, and they all feed into the construction of reasons. The most common of these is that adoption isn't meant to be an equivalent to having birth children. If you feel that adopting a child will never be the same as having your own birth child, then you are already on the right lines. Adopting *is* different, and adoptive families *are* different. Once men realise this, there's often a fundamental shift in their thinking. Adoption becomes a field of possibilities, rather than a substitute for something that cannot be. Adoption will not make childlessness go away, any more than it will undo the child's separation from her birth parents. It will not erase anything for any of the parties involved. But it will offer an alternative way forward for all of them. It creates a new path: a path that is unusual, intriguing, and full of potential rewards.

Long-term adoptive fathers frequently cite a single defining piece of information learned in preparation class that acted as a "breakthrough" insight. For some this is the recognition that no birth mother willingly gives up her child, and that every birth mother experiences a profound loss when her child is, for whatever reason, adopted. This knowledge may underpin the adoptive father's antagonism towards the concept of ownership of children. Other adoptive dads point to the idea that adoption is an imperfect solution for all the involved parties. The imperfection of the adoptive route, its acceptance of compromises and its triumphs over the random unfairnesses of life form a bulwark against creeping perfectionism on the part of any adoptive parent.

Control and perspective

Much of men's distress in the early stages of thinking about adoption relates to feelings about control. It's hard for men in our society to accept they cannot control certain things, such as fertility. Advertising and mainstream popular culture continue to push a worldview where we can each satisfy our own desires, as long as we buy the right products, work hard enough or "believe in ourselves". But biology doesn't know any of these truths.

Religious and philosophical practices influenced by Eastern thinking encourage the individual to let go of their illusionary need to control the world around them, and the same thinking informs the more practical forms of psychotherapy and counselling. Adopters with strong religious convictions seem to make better accommodations with the loss of control inherent in childlessness than those who lead a purely secular life.

The well-known opening of the Serenity Prayer, attributed to Reinhold Niebuhr (1932) but thought by some to have an earlier origin, and a mainstay of the Alcoholics Anonymous movement, was often quoted or alluded to by adoptive dads:

> **God grant me the serenity**
> **to accept the things I cannot change;**
> **courage to change the things I can;**
> **and wisdom to know the difference.**

Adopters need to be particularly aware that their children are likely to pose problems that will challenge the parental sense of control. They may, for example, have behaviours that anger or repel their new parents, but which are not going to disappear overnight. Indeed, a child's dysfunctional behaviour in the early part of a placement may get far worse before it gets better as she continues to test her new parents. Since begetting and ruling are the twin pillars of the traditional paternal role, most adoptive dads have little choice but to become "new men", if they were not before.

Adopters sometimes relate other life-experiences to the changes in thinking they experience during preparation and assessment. Prospective adopters are often in their late thirties or older, so they have entered the phase in life where they are likely to encounter tragedies amongst their family and friends. Illness, bereavement and divorce become realities of their own circle rather than abstract concepts. They may have friends who experience difficulties with their children, or even lose them. Life changes that are close to home help male adopters adjust their worldviews, and remind them that life doesn't usually work out the way it does in the ads. In fact, some men reported they had come to regard adoption as one of the more normal family situations in modern life rather than a peculiarity.

Talking into adoption

The single most important factor in their early approach to adoption mentioned by adoptive fathers is their ability to talk to as wide a range of people as possible. While many adoptive dads read the available books and consumed material from the web, the majority said talking to other people was the most helpful contribution to their learning. All kinds of people can be useful at this stage: family, friends, professionals and even random acquaintances. Sometimes the most important contributions someone can make to an adopter's early thought processes stem from their own ignorance about adoption. A friend's innocent remark about "getting a baby from an orphanage" or idle wonder whether "it will be the same as a real child" can quickly show a prospective adopter how far they have come in their own thinking.

More constructively, people who have already been through the adoption process are a valuable source of advice, humour and empathy. This book aims to pass on some of the experiences and insights of adoptive fathers, but there are other routes to this knowledge. Joining an organisation such as Adoption UK gives you access to other adoptive parents, and other prospective adopters. You can go to Adoption UK meetings in your local area, and question folks who have been through what you're going through. You will also be able to find all the permutations of the adoption situation within such an organisation, as well as meeting the extremes of experience. Being a member carries no obligations, but many benefits. Adoption groups are friendly, self-driven, open-minded collections of ordinary people who happen to find themselves with something in common.

Prospective adoptive fathers also find it useful to talk to "ordinary" dads too. Many childless men strenuously avoid listening to too much dad talk, and may feel embarrassed at suddenly expressing an interest in their friends' family lives, and their experiences of fatherhood. But men's most usual experience when approaching other dads for advice is overwhelmingly positive. Even fathers who have little or no informed opinion on adoption – in other words, most birth fathers – tend to welcome the opportunity to talk about fatherhood. In fact, non-adoptive fathers may get few opportunities to talk honestly and in depth about parenting with other guys, and you may find your arm being eaten off.

One of the reasons adoptive fathers benefit from talking to other men is the simple repetition of the basic truths of contemporary fatherhood. Most of us need to hear a message a number of times and in different ways before we take it in. Fathers generally repeat the same clutch of messages: children can make you more angry than you'd have thought possible, children constantly surprise you, children change so quickly, children are a delight but they're not easy. Every father couches these messages in a different way and has different ways of dealing with their implications.

Parenting is parenting. Being an adoptive parent is special in some ways but in other ways it's the same as everyone else. You have to remember it's about giving, not taking.
Adoptive father

Building new foundations: Preparing for adoption

> **In an ideal world, all parents would go through this before getting a certificate that allowed them to have kids.**
> Adoptive father

This chapter explores men's experiences of the assessment and preparation elements of the adoption process. The main topics are home study and preparation classes. The focus is on what men thought of the various elements of assessment and preparation and how they dealt with this part of the adoption journey.

Home invasion

The major part of a prospective adopter's assessment is carried out through what is known as a "home study". A series of interviews and discussions, the home study takes place over a period of several months and is used to gather all the material needed for the report that will recommend the applicant to panel. A social worker is assigned to the prospective adopters to undertake the home study and assessment. Approved adopters later meet social workers assigned to children for whom the plan is adoption.

Men find the home study an intense and unnerving experience. Excavating their own past to find clues to their understanding of the parental role is a novel and often uncomfortable task. Many men immediately draw a blank when they begin this task. As one social worker told me:

> **It's the first time for many men that they will ever have been asked about their histories, and many of them say they want to be more involved dads than their own fathers.**

The home study demands a combination of internal questioning and external scrutiny unprecedented in the experience of most men. Men are not generally used to articulating their feelings about their upbringing, and unaware that such feelings will ever be of interest to a social worker parked on their sofa. The home study relationship is not a therapeutic one, so although the social worker will support the process of introspection and interpretation, she cannot directly help to resolve any personal issues that might arise. Although home study sessions can be uncomfortable, and prospective adopters may feel their personal space is being invaded, it is vital that social workers interact with prospective parents in the place that will become a child's new home.

Some adoptive fathers mentioned it's best to accept the home study as part of the process, and not to take it too personally. This advice implies that some aspects of the home study do indeed strike very close to the heart, and, if handled wrongly, can provoke anger or sadness. Inevitably, discussing subjects like physical or sexual abuse of children while you are sitting at your dining table can be stressful. According to one prospective male adopter:

> **During the assessment your social worker is there, but then you're left with the new information for a few days. It tests your emotions . . . I never thought myself susceptible to these things.**

The other major aspect of the home study mentioned by men is their surprise at some of the practical challenges associated with adoptive family life. For example, some adopters discover they have widespread and supportive networks which will help greatly with the placement, while others come to the equally surprising conclusion that their immediate friends and family will not be of much practical help.

The most frequently mentioned part of the home study was the section of the old Form F that specified the adopters' restrictions with regard to potential matches. This was a long checklist presenting various types of children's backgrounds or problems, with spaces for the prospective adopters to indicate whether or not they felt they could consider such a child. Although every adopter approached the list differently, almost every adopter also found categories that caused them great distress to reject.

> **I found one part of the process extremely hard – what I called "playing God". At the end of the assessment we had to indicate the type of child we wanted – preferred age, preferred sex – and what we thought our capabilities were . . .**
> (Daniel, 2000)

The neutral language of the professionals talks of prospective adopters as "resources" to children, and this part of the old Form F was aimed squarely at specifying the exact nature of the resource the applicant was offering. For the applicants, however, this task felt like a process of serial rejection. Adopters saw themselves as consigning children in care to a continued life on the shelf. The disparity we've seen between adopters' approved ranges and children's needs evidenced by the reports of the National Register for England and Wales needs to be addressed by wider recruitment of adopters, continuing publicity about the needs of children needing adoption, and more flexible, child-centred approaches to matching. The new Form F therefore does away with this "box-ticking" page.

Comments made by many adoptive fathers suggest home study sessions can act accidentally as outlet valves for deep emotions. This phase of the process is acknowledged to be a very stressful life-stage for the adopters. Searchlights are trained on every area of the applicant's life, and for couples this includes their relationship with each other.

Most social workers and their clients acknowledge this stress is part of the overall plan. The system is not designed to offend or unhinge applicants as the press sometimes implies, though the shocked reaction of non-adopters to the assessment experiences of adopters and the rapid judgements that follow certainly make the process look harsh to outsiders. Adoption workers are not torturers: but, to an unprepared or vulnerable adoptive parent, *children* can be. Some social workers plainly see one function of the assessment phase as a way of pre-stressing the parents so they will neither buckle or crack in the face of the much greater challenges ahead.

The assessment process contains at least two areas of potential conflict arising from practical aspects of the task. These are self-assessment and competency-based assessment or "evidencing".

Self-assessment in the adoption context has a rather different meaning to that used by the Inland Revenue. While the tax collector wants to offload labour on to the consumer so the role of the authorities is to check rather than complete tax calculations, adoption agencies would be failing in their duty of care if they made applicants solely responsible for discovering their suitability as adoptive parents. The extent to which an applicant writes the social worker's report varies widely amongst agencies, and indeed amongst social workers within agencies. Some regard the applicant's contribution as a means of ensuring his committed attention to the process and its results, knowing white-collar workers especially are likely to treat a report-writing exercise with the utmost care. Other social workers believe they must control the entire process and that turning over too much labour to the applicant opens the door to potential error or deceit. Some social workers prefer to attach personal statements to the report, so the adopters' voices are heard in the submission to panel, although this justification is being eroded by newly guaranteed applicant access to panel attendance. However the social worker decides to manage the creation of the report, the final product will always be her responsibility.

Some adoptive fathers mentioned that their involvement in the creation of the report caused friction. Their concern here was not that they were being silenced, but that they were mistrusted. A couple contributing to their assessment report may express a degree of ownership over the process their social worker has to correct, and the man seems more likely to be angered by this intervention (or to recall his anger) than his partner.

Competence-based assessment is a recent attempt to objectify and standardise the way prospective adopters are assessed for their parenting capabilities. The majority of prospective adopters are childless couples who obviously cannot point to years of personal child care experience. The traditional approach to assessing competency in such cases is to draw on applicants' child care experiences in the extended family and amongst their friends, and to ask them how they would handle particular situations. As job recruiters know, asking someone how they *would* deal with an imaginary situation is a poor guide to their actual behaviour. We all have an understandable tendency to imagine ourselves doing the right thing. Asking people to identify real instances of behaviour from their own experience is a much surer route to understanding their abilities. The competencies section of the revised Form F includes a number of dimensions against which an applicant can be scored.

A sure tool for exposing and exploring parenting competencies in applicants with little child care experience is the practical exercise. These have not been used in any great volume by agencies, and I suspect many prospective adopters would be aghast at the idea of performing such an exercise. I offer my own experience: my partner and I undertook two exercises as part of our assessment. We took six-year-old twins up to London for the day; and we had a four-year-old stay with us for two days. Our agency did not supply the guinea pigs: we had to beg them off our friends. From the vantage point of several years later, these challenges seem laughably easy. At the time they seemed much harder, especially as we were required to plan each exercise and report back on it. Yet we were happy to accept we could hardly seek to make a lifelong commitment to a child if we were unwilling even to look after one for a short period.

Any man who is planning to seek to be an adopter is well advised to start acquiring child care experience as early as possible in the process. For childless couples who may have shunned the company of small children during painful years of fertility treatment, this can imply an abrupt turnaround in their behaviour. However, their child-blessed friends – preoccupied as they are with their own affairs – will probably not notice the sudden change of heart; and if they do they will exploit it mercilessly. Prospective adopters make excellent baby-sitters, tending to offer themselves as sitters and even dreaming up grownups-only treats that they insist their parenting friends are long overdue. Helping out with friends' families helps prospective adopters add to their evidence of competency, gives them opportunities to reflect on the differences between children with stable, loving homes and those who have been in care, and builds a bank of favour-points they can draw on when they become parents in their own right.

No laughing in class

The first time I heard the phrase "attachment theory", I assumed it had something to do with the correct use of the vacuum cleaner, and was some kind of euphemism for male domestic failure. But I wouldn't have dared say this in an adoption preparation class.

What men most commonly miss in the adoption preparation stage, and particularly in preparation classes, is humour (however feeble). The chances of a prospective male adopter asking for more laughs in a preparation class are, however, vanishingly small. There isn't much to laugh about in the details of child abuse, family breakdown and social policy.

The preparation stage exposes would-be adopters to material that is shocking and painful. It often inspires outrage in men, who are aghast at the crimes perpetrated so casually on children. They often become ashamed of their own ignorance of child abuse (in all its forms, through sexual, physical, emotional and neglectful) and guilty about their own relatively privileged childhoods. Adoptive dads talk of their realisation that their own lingering, adolescent complaints about the parenting they received pale into insignificance when they are confronted with case studies of typical children in the care system.

Yet humour is one of the tools men use to manage their emotions, and, crucially, to communicate with each other. The denial of humour in the adoption process hinders men from making potentially supportive relationships with each other. Men in a preparation group will often find a topic outside of adoption where they can talk safely and humorously, so they can get to know each other in a way that is comfortable to them. At some point one of them might tentatively question some of the terminology or points of view used in the training material, and then the others will jump in.

Men need to engage with unfamiliar material through challenge, and sometimes ridicule. This approach works in most areas of a man's life, and it works for adoption too. But it is very much a playground activity. There is little chance to challenge the material in preparation class, and perhaps little reason to. Where men do engage passionately with what they are being told, they often choose to do so through analytical challenge; for example, questioning the research that has been done into adoption outcomes.

That men own and come to terms with the facts of adoption is more important than the mode or venue in which they reach their understanding. However, designers of adoption preparation classes would do well to consider male learning styles as well as female ones, and to provide as much scope as possible for men to question and reframe the material being presented. It may even be worthwhile including separate breakout sessions for the men and women, during which each group considers how adoption will change their lives. This would give men the opportunity to start building the kind of support network women seem to build so naturally. Adoptive fathers who reported the use of male breakout groups in their preparation classes found them to be useful both for relaxing their defences and sharing viewpoints.

Sometimes, the only route to coming to terms with personally challenging material is through the doorway of humour. If you can laugh about something, then you can also cry: and then you can begin to move on. It seems we are always criticising men for either taking things too seriously (and going to war) or trivialising them (and going to the pub). It's this extremism that makes women shake their heads and agree that men "never grow up". But until men have more experience reflecting on their emotional styles and learning to choose how they react to information they find threatening, they will continue to use humour as a key alternative to denial.

Learning curves

The first surprise men commonly report from their preparation and assessment period is their confrontation with the meaning of identity. By the time we are adults, the fraught process of constructing our personalities is usually confined to memories of adolescence. We are free, independent people with rights and responsibilities and we rarely think particularly deeply about what it means "to be me".

But adoption confronts identity. Indeed, in the legal sense, adoption could be said to be wholly about identity, at least in the law's origins if not its current, more holistic, practice. Who are you, if you are removed from your family and installed in another family? Are you the person you were before? Do you become the person you were meant to be? Who are "your people"? Where do you belong?

The practical manifestation of this issue strikes initially in the subject of children's names. Should an adoptive parent change their child's given name? Renaming for the purposes of parental preference treats the child like a piece of decorative property. However, where children have unconventional names that may cause them problems with their peers, the new parents may be right to change the name to something more mainstream. 'It never occurred to me that anyone would name their child "Posh",' said one adoptive father.

From the point of view of the small child, their name is who they are. A child may think that if you change her name, you are actually destroying and recreating her; denying her past, and making her original identity a label for the taboo. Some children, with the insight and appetite for life many children in care show, see a change of name as a positive symbol of their onward movement in life. They may choose their own new name, and insist upon it. However, no parent or adoption worker can assume any specific child will take this attitude.

The complex relationship between labels and identities is the starting point in a series of fundamental adjustments that prospective adopters make in their thinking. The extent and depth of these areas of mental revision are challenging, and applicants need time to absorb the material to which they are being exposed and integrate it into their growing understanding of the adoptive family's life.

It is all too easy to characterise the preparation and assessment period as an imposition, and a struggle. The material adopters grapple with during their education is both novel and challenging. Prospective adopters are asked to analyse their motivations, question their abilities, and prove their competence. But there is an enduring upside to this requirement. One adoptive father summed up neatly what nearly all the adoptive fathers I spoke to hinted at: 'I know people who'd be better parents if they'd had to learn what I had to learn.'

While prospective adoptive dads often express dismay at the idea of attending "parenting classes" (which, by the way, adoption preparation classes are most definitely not), they usually come to appreciate what they learn during their preparation. They may value what they learn from other adopters as much, or more than, the formal material. But the majority say the chance to think about and discuss the realities of life as a parent helped them adjust to family life, and saved them much doubt and anxiety.

Adoptive parents are given the chance to prepare for family life, whilst most people who have birth children are understandably focused on the birth process. No one would seriously suggest to an expectant mother that she contemplate how she deal with a toddler's tantrum, or an adolescent's identity crises. Nor is the average expectant father examined on whether he will make a good male role model and share in domestic duties. Yet these are issues parents of all kinds have to face at some time or another, and they are not trivial.

Adoptive parents have certain issues simplified for them. For example, while the courts in various European countries (including Scotland) have banned or attempted to limit smacking, many adoptive parents recognise that the early abuse in their children's lives rules out any form of corporal punishment in the family. Adoptive parents also know that the special circumstances of their children's origins means they won't be able to be too precious when the time comes to discuss the mechanics of human reproduction.

Above all, adoptive parents enter family life with a guaranteed high state of awareness about the challenges – and rewards – of parenting. They are well informed about their own instincts and habits, and therefore less likely to surprise themselves or their children with unhelpful attitudes or behaviours. This does not, of course, mean they are somehow perfected as parents during this phase of the adoption process. Indeed, for many adoptive fathers the assessment and preparation stage serves to make them aware of the magnitude of the parenting task, and may cause them to set themselves unrealistically high standards.

Looking back on assessment

Adoptive fathers differ in their attitudes to the preparation and assessment phase depending on the length of time since it took place. "Fresh" adopters use the language of adoption professionals, speaking of "attachment", "grief" and "support". More seasoned adopters refer to the usefulness of their personal networks and often seem to have jettisoned the theory used during preparation. But this does not mean approaches to adoption preparation have failed – quite the reverse may be true. After all, the experienced car driver does not use the tricks of memory and habit he was taught when learning to drive, such as naming the pedals "ABC" in reverse.

Successful adopters internalise the theories and models they learn about in preparation classes, and rapidly begin to see them enacted in their new family life. They do not stop to think, for example, which stage of grief their child is experiencing, so they can mark it on a chart: they comfort the child, or try to move her on, or give her space to grieve, depending on their own judgement of what the child needs at that point. Without the preparation material, the adopters may well not recognise that newly placed children go through grief processes as real and as devastating as those that adults experience with bereavement. The fading of the theoretical details does not mean the material failed to stick.

Men recognise that most parents aren't tested for their suitability to be parents. The fact that adopters are subject to rigorous checks and extensive preparation is usually a surprise to people outside the adoption world – and that naturally includes most prospective adopters, at the early stages of their enquiry. However, it isn't too long before most men see the importance of assessment and preparation, and accept the workload and external attention the process entails.

As they progress further along the adoption journey, men often develop a positive attitude to the learning component of the process. While practically-minded men will think the best learning is that gained through experience, they will usually also recognise formal learning is useful too. Crucially, in the context of parenting a child, we need to recognise that not all experience is automatically good. A prospective adopter's experience of parenting is most often restricted to the parenting he himself received. He therefore necessarily has a restricted model of parenting, which urgently needs informing with additional material. Without this formal learning element, men run the risk of unwittingly re-enacting behaviours from their parents' repertoire they would rather not use, or that might be detrimental to their child's well-being.

The best-evidenced example of this issue is smacking. Some men maintain they have a right to chastise their children in any way they see fit – and may buttress this belief with the claim they were smacked as children "and it didn't do me any harm". It is pointless to dispute someone's assessment of their own early development. But it is not too hard to make someone see that a child who has been abused in early life is unlikely to respond to being hit by her new parent. One of the prime functions of adoption preparation is to remove automatic assumptions about how children should be cared for, in order to highlight the very special nature of the adoptive situation and underline the crucial influence of the adoptive parent on the child's onward development.

Several adoptive fathers commented they felt privileged to have been so thoroughly prepared for the wide range of challenges they might have to deal with as parents, beginning with issues of identity and running right through to managing relationships with their children as young adults. They may have chafed at the time, and wished for speedier progress, but many adoptive dads think their non-adoptive peers have missed out on some vital education, and have been sadly left to work with a restricted palette of parenting tools. There are undoubtedly non-adoptive parents who would benefit from parenting advice. After all, at the most dysfunctional end of the scale, parental incompetence can lead ultimately to care proceedings being instituted in regard to their children, and subsequently their adoption.

If this gives a somewhat smug image of the adoptive father several years down the line, smirking at the problems of his undereducated "breeder" friends, it's worth remembering this is a small and inconsequential form of superiority. And for most adoptive fathers, their attitude to their assessment is likely to remain one of tolerated ambiguity. As one adoptive father put it:

> **You're being assessed for a role you have no experience in – to take over from someone who demonstrably *can't***

> **perform that role, and that's difficult to get your head round.**

Many adoptive fathers deal with the ambiguities of assessment by regarding it as a kind of game or obstacle course. As long as the man is not seeking to falsify the process to get through it, experienced social workers are unlikely to condemn this attitude. After all, an ability to work with "the system" is a valuable attribute for adoptive parents, who will often need to act as advocates on behalf of their children. They may need persistence in getting special help for their child, recognition of her educational needs or in chasing compensation due to the child.

On the whole, while men usually start out seeing the assessment phase as an intrusive, long-winded liberty that has to be accommodated, they equally usually come to see it as a worthwhile process that makes them stronger. As the assessment phase continues, they begin to appreciate how the parts of the process fit together to ensure a rounded picture of the prospective adopters. And as the centrality of the child's interests takes root, they begin to appreciate the responsibility the agency's workers bear in approving adopters.

To panel

The assessment process ends with the submission of a recommendation to the agency's adoption panel. By the time the report is created, most applicants will be aware that they will be approved. Applicants who are clearly not going to be approved will usually be advised to withdraw from the process.

Few aspects of the assessment process are absolute barriers to approval. A conviction for offences against children will obviously act as an automatic bar, but most other crimes are looked at in the context of their occurrence and related to how the prospective adopter has since developed. On the health side, a chronic (that is, enduring) condition will not automatically disqualify the applicant; acceptance will depend on the effect of the applicant's condition on his ability to parent. Specialist opinion may be sought in such cases where GPs cannot rule on a particular condition.

Adoptive fathers tend to be anxious about "the checks", even when they know rationally they have nothing to fear. There is no other time in a person's life where their health, probity and financial security are simultaneously hauled up for examination and appended to an intimate account of their entire lives and intentions for the future. Applicants have no way of influencing the outcome of these searches, though they can of course appeal against any incorrect information produced by the checks. Given the current state of the relevant information sources, applicants are more likely to be troubled by the length of time taken for the checks to be completed than their actual results.

The opportunity for prospective adopters to attend the approval panel used to be discretionary but is now a right for all. Panel is a somewhat formal event, although those involved do their best to make it as friendly an experience as possible. The members of the panel review the information that has been submitted to them, and ask the prospective adopters any questions they may have.

Approved adopters rightly feel they have achieved a significant goal in passing their agency panel. But for many the journey is just starting. They now face a new period of confusion, delay, hope and despair: it's called "matching", but many adoptive fathers know it simply as "waiting".

6

Searching for children: The matching stage

Elinor Hardman

> **We want to get on with our lives.**
> Second-time adoptive father

"Matching" is the name given to the sometimes convoluted and often protracted period when a set of prospective adopters and prospective adoptees are identified as being suited to each other.

There are many ways a match can be brought about. Some adoption agencies practise concurrent planning, whereby children in care are matched with adopters during the preparation and assessment phase. In these cases a placement starts after the adopters have been approved, but with the child's legal status remaining as in-care. Concurrent planning provides the greatest security for the future of the child, since it creates a range of alternative routes. However, from the point of view of the prospective adopters, concurrency means there's a chance the child may not be freed for adoption, and that the adopters will "lose" the child to her birth parents. In practice, this happens very rarely. But for those adopters who do experience it, it is obviously a painful event. They need to be robust enough to recognise the overwhelming advantage to the child of returning to her birth family.

Adopters who are offered concurrent planning do have a significant advantage over adopters whose identification of their adopted child is delayed. Knowing who their children will be, the prospective adopters can begin to focus on the needs of their children very early on. Their preparation period can therefore be much more focused, with the children's needs dictating their actions before the placement begins.

For most adopters, potential adoptees will be unknown until after their approval panel. On approval, prospective adopters are usually required to give their approving agency a set period to find a match before they can look elsewhere. Why is this so? Is it just to allow the agency the administrative time needed to process the details of the children they have waiting to be adopted?

In the case of local authorities, the hold-off period achieves an economic aim. This is to ensure the authority gets first shot at using the resource it has invested in, namely the newly approved adopter.

It clearly makes sense for the authority to match its own adopters with adoptees wherever it can. However, some adoptions today must be made across local authority boundaries in order to ensure the safety of the child in her new home area. Safety can even be an issue in large counties, where popular central venues such as shopping centres offer opportunities for security risks. The authority may therefore not be able to make a match within its own area, even if other criteria suggest a good match.

If a match is not made within the hold-off period, adopters are free to seek matches elsewhere. Authorities vary in their support for adopters at this stage. They are obliged to enter the adopters' details in the National Register for England and Wales launched in 2001 and made fully operational in April 2002. Adoption workers may also use their contacts at other agencies to seek matches, but this activity will only take place if they have time. If an adopter approved by one local authority is ultimately "used" by another authority for a placement, then the approving authority will be paid a fee by the authority making the placement. However, achieving these fees is unlikely to be a high priority in the social services department, which has so many other tasks to perform. Adopters may also consider the listings of children who need adopting in the magazines published by BAAF and Adoption UK.

Adopters who use independent adoption agencies generally have an easier time with matching. This is because such agencies are usually organised on a national basis, giving them a wider reach and a fuller picture of the needs of children awaiting adoption. Independent adoption agencies have a proactive approach to matching that is not always present within local authority social services departments, who have many other priorities – priorities that may change according to political pressures. For example, at the time of writing, local authorities are reorganising to improve child safety and protection procedures following the findings of the Victoria Climbié Inquiry, which found that poor co-ordination amongst different professionals and agencies can result in tragic failures of care.[1] The reorganisation and refocusing is of course welcome, but it may mean there are fewer resources in the social services team to support approved adopters who cannot be matched within the authority's boundaries.

The uncertainty of the matching period can also be made more bizarre when competition breaks out between prospective adopters. Approved adopters learn about a potential match from their social worker, only to learn soon afterwards that one or more other sets of adopters are also being considered. None of the "competing" parties has chosen to do battle, and most people who find themselves in this situation react with frustrated dismay. None of the potential adopters can press their own case. It's up to the child's social workers to assess the candidate adopters, and to decide to meet one or more sets of candidates – assuming any of them make the grade.

Prospective adoptive fathers often find this situation hard to stomach. Most men submit to the adoption process with the attitude that any open process can be worked with, however tardy or painful it may prove to be. Where there is competition for a match, the fact the adopters' hands are tied can be hard for men especially to take. Add to this the fact that they have been readied to fight for their child's needs, and to be their advocate, and it becomes obvious some men are going to become angry or depressed at this turn of events.

Men with a managerial mindset will want to know what criteria are being used to judge the various applicants; and these men will suspect they are being fobbed off when given anodyne answers such as "whether or not it looks like a good match". All the adopter's insecurities about his suitability as a parent are likely to be rekindled. He may gloomily conclude that "his" children will be allocated to someone with a smarter house, or a bigger salary, or nicer teeth. And amidst all this worry, adopters are likely to lose any sense of the reality of the actual children for whom the matching

[1] www.victoria-climbie-inquiry.org.uk

decision is being made.

Prospective adopters frequently "lose" children. There are the children for whom they are candidate matches, but not the "winners". Then there are the potential adoptees they might be asked to consider during their search, working from the completed information about the child. It's here prospective adopters meet Form E, the counterpart to the Form F they have slaved to complete during their assessment. Form E details the background and needs of the child. Although the form is in a standard format, the quality of completed forms varies wildly. Standards often differ within agencies, depending on the individual who completed the form. Some Form Es are so bland as to be useless, and raise suspicions about the department's knowledge of the child being described. (In fact, most adopters report they learn far more from their child's foster carers when they eventually meet than they do from even the best completed Form E.)

The factor all Form Es have in common is that they are distressing to read. The abstract, categorised conditions that may apply to a child in care as discussed during preparation classes and home study sessions come starkly to life through genuine case notes. Sorrow, outrage and despair are common reactions to the details presented in Form Es. Prospective adopters may also feel a resurgence of generalised guilt that they cannot "save" all the abused children of the world, or that they lived for so long in ignorance of the horrors that are sadly so common in our community.

Outside of the concurrent planning system, it's impossible to predict how any one matching period will progress. For every family matched immediately there will be another with a tale of repeated losses. However, every adoptive family clearly gets over this hurdle. And when they do, and the placement starts, the matching period rapidly subsides into a vague memory. It may not be much comfort to adopters trapped in the matching stage to be told "everything will work out".

Men especially chafe at their powerlessness during this stage. To protect fragile male sanity while the matching misery continues, it's worth taking as much practical action as you can. Adoptive dads-to-be usually have their hands full making changes to the house, perhaps installing stairgates or assembling beds, painting rooms and yanking out poisonous plants. They can also burn off excess energy by managing as much of the matching process as they can, perhaps creating a "flier" to describe the adoptive couple that can be circulated to agencies. This is also a good time to attend to hobbies and interests you want to maintain in your new life. By continuing to go to the gym or fishing, you demonstrate to yourself your persistence and self-care during a period of otherwise awesome stress.

Concurrent planning

Concurrent planning is relatively new to the UK, with initial pilots now being gradually extended as experience with the approach grows. With the concurrent planning approach, the prospective adopters meet with the birth parent or parents at the start of the process. The child is then placed with the adopters in a fostering relationship, with formal adoption coming later. Concurrent planning eliminates the potential chain of changes that can happen in conventional settings, where a child may live with a succession of foster carers.

Concurrency can also be a less conflicted situation for the birth parent, who can experience the commitment of the adopters at first hand and participate in the constructive planning of their child's onward journey. Many children indicated for concurrent planning come from families where severe mental illness or addiction reduces their chances of adequate, safe care to nil. Such children are often identified before they are born, since the family is already known to social services. Concurrent planning is therefore a good route for adopters who want to adopt a baby rather than an older child.

To date three concurrent planning projects have been set up in

England, and progress is beginning to be reported for the first users of the schemes. The Manchester Adoption Society's Goodman Team stresses the main priority for any child in their scheme is to get them home to their birth parents, with adoption being "Plan B":

> **Joint recruitment is undertaken with the Adoption team and we find that many prospective carers choose the adoption route as it is less legally uncertain, is less stressful and involves less contact with the birth family. What draws carers to the Goodman Team is the realisation that drift, delay and repeated moves are unhelpful to children, the hope that a child placed will be less damaged, may be younger and have fewer problems in life due to their difficult beginnings[2].**

The Goodman Team's first cohort of ten carers has experienced only one case where the child returned to the birth parent. In four cases, the birth parents voluntarily relinquished the child. In three cases, the birth parents opposed the plan for adoption but did not object to the prospective carers themselves, whom they had of course met repeatedly during the concurrent planning process.

The Coram Family concurrent planning project (in London) has seen one child returned from a set of 18 placements, while the programme at Brighton and Hove has seen no child return to his or her birth parents from a total of 16 placements. Concurrent planning was first introduced by Lutheran Social Services in Seattle, Washington, USA nearly 20 years ago, and this project has experienced a nine per cent return rate from around 170 placements.

There is clearly a risk for the adopters that they will lose the child placed with them in a concurrent planning regime. One prospective

[2] http://www.manadopt.u-net.com/concurrent.htm

adoptive father identified here the head-versus-heart theme that underlies so much of the adoption journey: 'We understand intellectually that we could lose the child, but emotionally you don't know what it would be like.'

Probabilities

There is no possible route to adoption that completely eradicates risk, and given human beings' notoriously poor ability to assess probabilities, perhaps this is a good thing. The odds of winning the UK's national lottery are 14m to one, while the odds of an asteroid hitting the earth are a mere 20,000 to one. Yet most of us choose to believe in the likelihood of the first event over that of the second. We don't deal with probabilities rationally, but take them personally.

Our inability to process probabilities correctly may be a useful protective strategy for adopters. The knowledge that one in five placements fails, or that around one in 20 concurrent planning placements reverts, is likely to be interpreted as an external outcome: something that will happen to somebody else. Believing you are going to be successful is a better state of mind than a focus on failure, in any undertaking.

Couples who have been through fertility treatment will find the process of assessing probable outcomes wearily familiar. However, the reported rates of successful placements is very much more favourable to the adopters than any fertility clinic's statistics for live births. Although adoption is not a replacement for having a birth child, adopters will not fail to make a comparison between these outcome scenarios. For the gambler, concurrent planning is an attractive bet – but still a bet. For the child, concurrent planning is the least risky approach to ensuring her future well-being.

Matching children, mismatching workers

"Matching" is an active word, but most men's experience of this phase is of a vacuum punctuated by false alarms. It's therefore no surprise that their often fragile relationships with social workers are a key concern at this time. It is as though conflict and distrust flood in to supply some emotional interest during a period characterised by an absence of apparent progress.

Standards of competence differ in every profession, and social work is no different. However, since adopters are engaged in a project of a highly personal nature, and are grappling with issues that can have lifetime consequences for themselves and their children, perceived inadequacies on the part of social workers can cause acute distress in adopters. This is especially true for adopters who are used to the world of work, and even more so for the many middle-class adopters who have had management responsibilities.

Men in particular are often upset at the varying quality of the social workers they meet during the matching phase and beyond, sometimes becoming angry at what they perceive as poor service to the children within the worker's nominal care. A lack of any power over the social worker or her department adds to the frustration. Some adoptive fathers find themselves writing letters of complaint to the relevant department, often with the knowledge all they are doing is letting off steam.

The variations adoptive fathers most often report are related to social workers' experience of adoption. During the assessment and preparation stage, adopters hopefully build an agreeable working relationship with their appointed social worker. Even where the chemistry is not quite right, or the adopters suspect their social worker has less than stellar ability, the bounded duration of the assessment period and its focus on practical matters normally makes the relationship at least productive.

However, when the matching phase begins, adopters are exposed to social workers from elsewhere in the department, and from other authorities. They now meet social workers who may seem to have only a vague knowledge of the children whom they are representing.

More worryingly, such social workers may show scant knowledge of the adoption process, and of good practice. Occasionally, a child's social worker will seem antagonistic to the very idea of adoption, a stance that will bewilder and deflate the prospective adopter.

Since adoption is a statistical rarity in the overall workload of social services department, it's indeed possible that a child's social worker will have no direct personal experience of moving a child into an adoptive placement. Even where a social worker has been involved in adoption before, the event may have taken place some years previously. In addition, some social workers will have had few adoption-related contacts outside their own local authority.

Anecdotal evidence suggests social workers are capable of making the kinds of gaffes that would be kindly corrected in an adopters' preparation class. In one case a child's social worker suggested to the prospective adopters the only way to judge a match between them and the child would be to put them together and see what happened. This practice is unheard of in the UK, where the most contact a prospective adopter will have with a matched child is via a photograph or perhaps home video. Adopters learn in preparation class they are not at liberty to "try out" a child, but must be committed to her placement before meeting the child.

Other reports suggest social workers are often poorly informed about the children who are the topic of the proposed match. They may arrive for a meeting with the prospective adopters without notes, and fail to answer any specific questions about the child. Since these meetings almost invariably occur in the adopters' home, the adopters often form the view the social worker has come merely to judge them, according to some silent criteria.

The real reason for social worker reticence may indeed be their poor knowledge of the children under discussion, but it may also reflect the worker's need to study the potential parents. The prospective adopters are keyed up to learn about the child who may be placed with them; for them, this meeting may be the culmination of a very long and arduous process. They are naturally focused on learning as much as possible about the child, and can see the social worker as a barrier.

But, from the social worker's point of view, she is at the meeting to confirm the suitability of the adopters. The specific details of the child's personality, for example, will probably not affect her judgement. And if she spends too much time describing the child, she risks selling (or failing to sell) the child to the adopters. Her job is not to persuade the adopters to choose this child as their own, but to secure the best possible placement for the child for whom she is responsible. This is not a light matter. A social worker's apparent reluctance to talk in depth about the child usually indicates professional probity rather than hostility or incompetence.

Some social workers say their colleagues who manage adoptions of children in their care are being given "the nice end of the job", with the implication that these professionals have earned themselves a cushy number after a lifetime of less pleasant tasks. It may please some social workers to work with clients who are generally polite, definitely law-abiding and probably eager to please, as most prospective adopters inevitably are. It's also rewarding to see a child move into a successful placement and go on to be a happy part of a functioning family. But placing children for adoption is as challenging as any other area of social work, albeit in sometimes less obvious ways. Approving the placement of a child is a heavy responsibility, not an automatic process.

The two-way nature of the information flow in the matching period can easily mislead adopters into thinking they are the decision-makers at this stage. They are looking at candidate children and trying to decide whether they can meet each child's needs. Inevitably, their hopes, dreams and fears for their family play a part in their thinking. But although they may be making selections in their own minds, the child's social worker will discount this process. She doesn't need to be interested in the adopters' preferences, except insofar as they may reveal their motivations as parents and expose any potential weaknesses. While the information flow at matching time should be two-way, the matching decision will always be taken by the child's team, not the adopters.

Adoptive fathers sometimes complain that, once they are approved as adopters, they should no longer be subjected to questioning or doubted as to their suitability as parents. They see the approval of their adoption panel as a kind of driving licence. From the point of view of a child's social worker, however, an adopter's approved status does not remove her responsibility, which is to the child. And there are, after all, plenty of people with driving licences who are nevertheless a menace on the roads. No amount of credentials can shortcut the matching decision. Adoption is the most important and most protracted job interview a man will ever face.

Male adopters tend to have absorbed the same pop psychology as anyone else, and will apply it to themselves sometimes seriously and sometimes wryly. One adoptive dad told me "men sit in caves and focus, women want to talk about their feelings" and related this to his sometimes impatient approach to the process. Like many prospective adoptive fathers, this man wanted his agency to give him measured guidelines for phases of the process, and was frustrated not to get them. Men – especially those used to being in positions of authority and responsibility – often learn to structure their thinking around forecasts and goals. They need to hear figures for the average time taken for matching, for example, even though they will accept that such figures cannot be used as a guide for any particular case.

One social worker described how prospective adopters in the matching phase benefit from regarding their position as a point on a line they cannot currently see. Their children are on another line, and at some stage in the future the lines will meet. This is a particularly helpful image for those who are goal-oriented and used to planning horizons. It's a way of visualising one's faith in the eventual resolution of the situation, and a useful reminder that the child's journey is a salient factor as well as the adopter's. Men

Figure 1: Converging life-paths. An adopter's search may briefly intersect with the histories of many children before he meets his match.

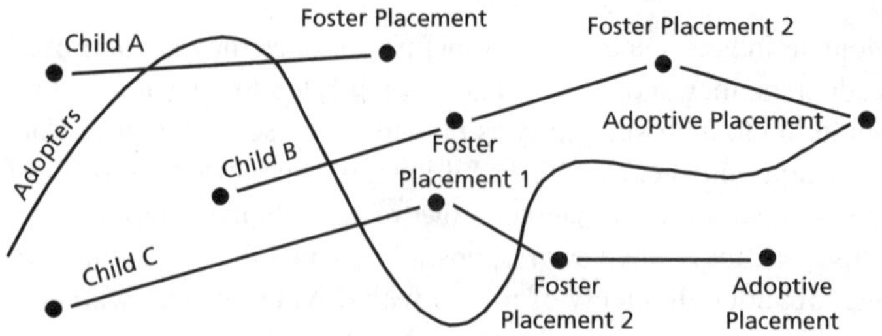

may not take too kindly to platitudes such as "it'll all work out in the end" but warm more readily to an idea of converging life-paths.

Matchmade: Expectant adoptive fathers

"Expectant fathers" have been blessed with their own medical condition, *couvade*. This is the French term for sympathetic pregnancy, whereby the partner of a pregnant woman experiences physical and emotional symptoms similar to those of the women. Some birth fathers note that, while they do not experience hormonal changes, they do go through behavioural changes. Couvade is not taken particularly seriously in the medical community. But the role of the father as an assistant to the mother during pregnancy and at the delivery is generally upheld. The modern habit is to encourage expectant fathers to present themselves during pregnancy but accept a secondary role.

Birth fathers often point gratefully to the period of pregnancy as a time during which they could get used to the idea of impending fatherhood, and to some extent let go of their old lives. Of course, pregnancy is not without its worries, and the birth father also experiences a range of hopes and fears during the term, often accompanied by feelings of helplessness. But the period of preparation in pregnancy, and the moment of change in childbirth, is now shared by men, and this seems to have improved men's sense of involvement in and commitment to their families.

Expectations of prospective adoptive fathers are rather different. Although the male partner may be destined to be the secondary carer in the family, he remains, fairly or not, the putative chief risk to the child with whom the adopters have been matched. His commitment to the new family is therefore studied with equal intensity as that of his partner. For the approved male adopter who is "expecting", willingly taking a reduced role is not an option.

Men with pregnant partners may find it hard to share in the pregnancy, and little advice is offered to them as to how they can participate during this time – other than by being "supportive". Although they see images of the growing foetus from regular scans and attend antenatal classes, birth fathers are still largely excluded until the moment of birth itself. Adoptive fathers, on the other hand, are expected to be as involved as their female partners during the assessment, preparation and matching phases. Their parallel to birth is the first meetings with the child to be placed with them, and these meetings may stretch out over one or more weeks. Adoption workers will focus more on the needs of the primary carer in any couple, but will also recognise that the practical involvement of the secondary carer is a vital component in the placement's success.

But, owing to a marked fall-off in external attention after an adoption order is made, the adoptive father may reduce his involvement in the family to the level expected in a "normal" family – whatever that might be. This is less an indication that adoptive fathers are forced to play a full part only while professionals are observing them and more a reflection of the way new families settle into mainstream patterns of behaviour. Indeed, many adoption workers will stress the importance of the adoptive father's returning to work and behaving like other fathers, so that he gives an appropriate male role model. As adoptive fathers become more experienced in their role, and more confident of their abilities and judgement, they will generally seek their own participation comfort zones.

The assessment and preparation phase of the adoption process does not really mirror pregnancy. Nor is the "miracle of childbirth" quite the same thing as the bizarre moment when an adopter meets his children for the first time.

The major difference between pregnancy and the pre-adoption period is the bounded nature of human gestation. Partners of pregnant women know the pregnancy will end at some point, and hope that it does so at around nine months with the birth of a healthy baby. Adopters can rarely predict if or when their children will "arrive". One adoptive dad said the adoption process 'took 18 months, which is about twice the time you'd be pregnant'. Others may total their years spent pursuing fertility treatment, reviewing their options and travelling along the adoption path and present an "adoptive pregnancy period" of many years. The common difficulty all adopters face is the unknowability of the curve they are moving along.

However, once a match has been approved, the adoption timeline compresses abruptly. Prospective adopters who have been thinking about wide ranges of possible children and perhaps investigating several potential matches suddenly know the name of their child, and the date they will meet her. A bewildering universe of possibilities collapses down to a differently bewildering certainty.

Once a match is approved by the child's local authority, events normally happen swiftly. The child's social worker will be keen to have her moved out of care as quickly as reasonably possible. Social workers will take into account the needs and circumstances of the foster carer, recognising that foster carers will be helping prepare the child to move. Social workers also respect existing arrangements within foster families, so moves may be delayed to allow for booked holidays. There is a general antipathy towards moving children over the Christmas break, since Christmas is an emotionally stressful time for families. With these caveats accepted, a matched adopter will experience a sudden redefinition of their previously hazy calendar. Many find themselves contemplating a three-week "pregnancy".

Adoptive fathers therefore have to squeeze their "expectancy" into a very short period. They are likely to feel a mixture of relief that one period of uncertainty has come to an end, and excitement (or fear) about the new age about to dawn. There is little opportunity to indulge in any "couvades", especially since there are no outward signs that the adopters' lives are about to change. Prospective adopters carry invisible bulges, and can't hope to be offered seats on buses.

This situation makes male adopters somewhat anachronistic. Despite the length of their struggle to become parents, the actual granting of their parental status is, in effect, more or less instantaneous. The act of matching and the placement of the child happen so close together in time that adoptive fathers can be said to have perfected the stereotype of the begetting-only father. For once in the adoption process, consequences follow swiftly upon actions. They may have had months or even years to get used to the idea of adoptive parenthood, but they may only be given a few days to come to terms with the reality of the *specific* child for whom they will be responsible, and with whom they hope to fall in love.

> **My step-kids don't need me so much because they're grown up. But the little ones . . . We're their hope in life. I feel something inside me.**
> Stepfather and adoptive father

7

Placement and displacement: Men meet their children

We've been doing some regression stuff, feeding him with a bottle. It's good for the nutrition and the hugs. He loves Rock-a-bye Baby . . . The first time I sang it, he just stared at me. It was like a non-verbal "wow!".
Adoptive father

In adoption "placement" is the term used to describe the period when a child lives with her new parents prior to legal adoption. The hope of every placement is that it will convert into a successful lifetime family situation. This chapter explores how men approach the placement, including the initial meetings with their children.

Introductions

Once a match is approved, a planning meeting will be held for the adopters to agree with the child's agency how and when they will meet with the child. This period is known as "introductions". The introductions period for a pre-school child can last anywhere between a week and three weeks, depending on the circumstances of the child and her social worker's assessment of her needs during the transition. Introductions can last much longer for an older child, or be much shorter for a baby.

The first meeting between the matched child and the adopters is generally kept brief and low-key, with subsequent daily sessions lengthening the contact and enabling the new parents to become familiar with all aspects of the child's routine. The first part of the introductions therefore usually takes place in the foster home.

The foster home

The child at the centre of the adoptive placement is generally discussed and reported upon in terms of her life story to date, and her needs for the future. Her current environment, which will almost certainly be a foster family, will tend to be touched on lightly within the documentation. However, this is the place where you will meet your adoptive child for the first time, and where the first part of your life together will be spent.

If the general public have somewhat vague ideas about what adoption involves, our ignorance about fostering is even more profound. In fact, many people do not know there is a difference between fostering and adoption, assuming these are two names for the same thing. Those who know that foster carers look after children temporarily while other solutions are found for their long-term well-being may still be under the illusion that foster parenting is a lucrative career. Although fostering is being continually professionalised through training and standardisation of practices, foster carers will give a wry smile if you suggest that they are recompensed in any lavish manner for the vital work that they do. Being the good souls that they are, they are unlikely to yell at you. The motivations of foster carers is too large a subject for this book: suffice it to say that in the overwhelming majority of cases, adopters meet committed, organised and loving foster families who contribute massively to the stability, happiness and long-term life chances of their charges.

However, the very competence of most foster carers can be alarming for adopters with little child care experience. A busy, child-centred home decorated with the pictures of the children who have been a part of the family at one time or another can present a stark contrast to the lives of the adopters, who may just have left the smell of fresh paint in the nursery and a single photograph of the child they hope will become a part of their lives. Knowing the carers currently looking after your child have done every child-rearing task a million times over can be daunting. They may have fostered literally dozens of children.

None of us is an expert in every human activity. Your ability to parent will have been rigorously examined during your adoption assessment, and now is the time to engage your faith in the validity of the assessment system. If you do find yourself feeling daunted in the foster home, it's worth remembering the world is awash with people who are "better" than ourselves. It's just that we rarely invite ourselves over to their homes to watch how they do it, eat their food, disrupt their routine – and then walk away with one of their family members. Competent parents litter the earth, and you will soon join their number.

It is easy to fall under the spell of a foster family, and begin to believe that, even if you can match them for basic parenting competence, you cannot transform children in the way you may believe the foster carers have done. Yet the belief that foster carers regularly work miracles is unfair to yourself, and to foster carers themselves. Foster placements can effect great changes in a child's health and happiness simply by replacing a dysfunctional family environment with a stable one. They also play an important role in preparing children to move on to adoption.

The key difference between the foster carer's role and the adoptive parent's is that the adopter works from a long-term timeframe, whereas the foster carer's outlook is necessarily more short-term. Problems that are contained within the foster setting may be candidates for more serious intervention within the adoptive family. Specific therapies, for example, may not be embarked on during the foster placement because their success will rely on months, and possibly years, of repeated treatment. Since an adoptive placement will often take a child across an administrative boundary, and sometimes great distances across the country, interventions that may be disrupted may not be started at all. In addition, there may not be the funding available within the fostering budget to address such needs. Finally, where the plan for a child is adoption, carers and their managers are understandably reluctant to embark on any course that may be seen as intrusive or pre-emptive by the eventual adopters. For all these reasons, children in care have their basic and legal needs met, and receive the love and personal, constructive attention any child needs. There is much more the adoptive parent must add to the mix. A child will have received all the inoculations she needs, but may not have been referred for speech therapy. She may be attending a pre-school group, but not necessarily the one that the adopter would have chosen for her.

The introductions period can easily be a time when adopters feel a loss of control over the adoption process. Their lives are taken over by an often complex timetable of visits, collections and routines as they try to learn about the child and her needs. New adopters who begin to feel inadequate in the department of heroics when faced with the busy reality of a foster family may find it helpful to start looking for the longer-term issues their child faces, and how the new family might start to accommodate or resolve these. This helps the new parents to shift their attention to the future, and plays to successful adopters' constructive tendencies. Children in care are, in many senses, in a holding pattern. An adoptive placement breaks this pattern and introduces a new phase of permanency.

First encounters

Many adoptive fathers (and mothers too) gradually forget the details of the introductions period. I was lucky to catch a few men close to their introductions, and found a number of similarities in their reports. First, men noted the introductions plans generally changed during the period, with a slightly faster move to the placement home being quite common. It seems where the introductions are going well, with the children well prepared for their move and all the involved adults giving the right kind of signals, children tend to want to move to their new homes soon after they have seen the house and given it their approval.

Perhaps surprisingly, given the insistence on the adopters' home as the venue for home study, introductions plans always call for the first part of the period to be held at the foster home. This makes sense, since this is the child's home, and the proposed parents must be introduced gently into her life. Yet it's also hard to believe a child can really trust a candidate parent who seems, at least for the first few days, to have no home of their own.

Second, men mention their surprise at the lack of professional support received during the introductions period. It seems most agencies step back after the introductions plan has been formulated, and leave its execution to the adopters and foster carers, with perhaps regular phone calls to check on progress, and a midpoint review session. Clearly no one else can do this part of the process: it's the moment of truth for the adopters as they embark on the "real" part of their journey. Yet the contrast with the previous period of close professional attention is stark. 'Everybody disappeared,' said one adoptive dad. Adopters who have believed themselves to be grudgingly putting up with their social worker suddenly wish she was there with them 24 hours a day.

Third, it seems differences of one kind or another tend to crop up between foster carers and the adopters. Many of these quickly become trivial in hindsight. For example, an adoptive dad may feel a foster dad is being unnecessarily critical of the adoptive home, or clinging to the child. It's hardly surprising if two families, colliding at random through a shared interest in helping a particular child, find they don't see eye to eye on every matter. But it's worth remembering that the introductions period does not last forever, and that if the placement is to work, then the foster carers' influence will wane.

Memory tends to crystallise and tidy situations that were originally fraught with ambiguity and confusion. Many adoptive fathers report their experiences of meeting their children-to-be as sharp vignettes, but vignettes with more complex subtexts. Adoptive dads often say the strength and immediacy of their feelings for the child on first meeting surprised and even overwhelmed them.

Some adoptive fathers also mention their partners were more circumspect than themselves. Perhaps men are "softer" than we give them credit for. Or perhaps it's just the positive feelings remain as the apex of a welter of mixed emotions when memory gets to work on rationalising the experience. When questioned, adoptive fathers often admit to a great deal of apprehension around the first meeting. It may be that the treasured memories of first contact gain some of their piquancy from the relief that accompanies the first encounter of the prospective new family.

The strangeness of the introductions period lingers with all adoptive fathers. Though the emotional power of the period fades with time, its unique flavours remain and are never diluted to blandness. People outside adoption are often keen to believe adoptive families rapidly become "normal" and will say, as if to reassure themselves, that "you're just like any other family". But healthy adoptive families do not deny the randomness, pain and regret in their lives. For the parents to do so would be to imply the children should also deny their pasts. This is not to say adoptive families regularly bemoan their situation: they rather tend to celebrate their formation, recognising the complexity of the situation and giving thanks for its many positive attributes.

Adoptive fathers can therefore be frank in remembering their earliest feelings about their children, in ways that may cause non-adopters discomfort. One adoptive father said cheerfully how ugly he found his adopted baby son – though it was also clear how quickly they had developed an incredibly strong relationship. Another adoptive dad summarised the bewilderment of many men during the introductions phase, saying 'you're thrown together with these people you have nothing in common with'. Although a lifetime's relationship lies ahead, the strangeness of those first moments can never be airbrushed from the picture. They add a unique piquancy to the adoptive father's experience.

Clicking

The term "bonding" is frowned on amongst adoption professionals, because its precise meaning doesn't apply to the adoption relationship. "Bonding" is, according to the experts, a one-way process in which a baby recruits its mother as its lifeline. Adoption workers prefer to talk about "attachment", since it is a two-way process in which both people seek to create a relationship with each other. Attachment is also a process that can occur at other stages in life as well as infancy, and it can persist over a much longer period than bonding. It's also a more complex process whose progress is sometimes halting, and usually difficult to assess. The word "attachment" is, unfortunately, most often followed by the term "disorder", since failures of attachment are a primary focus for failed adoptive placements.

Nevertheless, the introductions period naturally creates opportunities for new family members to make sudden connections with each other. These often occur with great emotional force, so it's not surprising some people regard these connections as evidence of deep bonding. It might be more characteristic of their random nature and perhaps transitoriness to call these events signs that the parties are "clicking". Small connections, such as a shared smile or an unsolicited offer of a toy, can be the grit around which the early pearl of a new family is created.

At the same time, these connections can be upsetting, as can their absence. New adoptive parents are frequently confounded by their inability to understand the speech of young children, while their foster families have no such trouble. Of course, no adult can instantly tune in to a small child's peculiarities of speech; but the momentous sense of occasion that can adhere to the introductions phase can cause new parents to lose sight of this fact.

The most important resource the new family has is time: the time that it will spend together, building relationships and creating a new life together. That quality of time is in short supply during the introductions period, where even the best designed timetable is still a timetable. Many parents report that "normality" only begins to set in once the child has moved into her new home permanently, and the family can spend some serious time doing what all people need to do in order to become comfortable with each other: nothing.

Support during the introductions period

The introductions phase is one of many unusual, yet widely experienced, passages in the life of an adoptive family. It is the first time the theoretical business of becoming a parent to a child in care collapses to a real time, space – and child. Despite the preparation the parents will have done, both at the general level and with particular attention to the child who will be placed with them, the minutes, hours and days that make up the introductions period are immensely stressful. Children who have been presented through paper forms that necessarily focus on the circumstances that brought them into care and thereafter into adoption planning, now materialise in flesh and blood, and in the setting of an unknown family home. The adoptive parents are now responding to the realities of the child in real time. Some men find the transition from the adult business of meetings and paperwork to face-to-face time with the child unnerving, and all the more so since this is supposed to be the aim of the process.

The physical and emotional stress of this period should not be underestimated. Adopters may have to travel long distances to visit their child, and the need to be present when she wakes up or goes to sleep can make for long days. Even local placements require complex logistics, especially if the adoptive parents are juggling work obligations as well. This is a period when adoptive dads do well to take extended time off work.

The many comings and goings of the introductions period exact an emotional toll from everyone involved. When introductions are going well, each day's parting can seem like a cruel and inexplicable loss to both child and adopters. Introduction plans are sometimes shortened when the stress on the child is judged to be too great and an earlier moving-in date would help the transition.

The introductions phase, and the beginning of the placement, inevitably generate a lot of shopping. You may think you are well prepared, but chances are that many vital purchases will have been necessarily delayed until you have met the child. Older children, for example, need to be consulted on how their bedrooms will be decorated. This can make for a good first joint project as a new family – but it also burns up time and energy.

Adoptive parents need the support of their networks during this phase. Friends and family are best used to fetch and carry, and even discreetly deliver meals, while otherwise keeping as much in the background as possible.

Dads and introductions

The situations and experiences we have discussed so far apply in equal measure to both adoptive mums and dads. However, men in couples may be more alert to some of the effects because the key focus is often on the adoptive mother. Where the mother is to be the primary carer, it is unsurprising if her response to the child and the development of their relationship gain more attention. Lacking the drama of childbirth, men's anxiety in the introductions phase has no focus.

Adoptive dads may find it useful to concentrate on being *there* during this period. This is a time to make an impression. It's not sensible to overwhelm the child, or act in any way that feels out of character. But you must be a hundred per cent "on" during the visits. Your child deserves the opportunity to learn as much as possible about you as early as possible, so that she may draw her own conclusions about your safety and suitability. The smallest baby needs exposure to your smell and smiles.

Dads should also be prepared to be punched, jumped on, and strangled – and not just by boys. Physical play of this kind is one of the most basic ways that children "test" adults who are cast in the role of carer. They want to know if you can take the knocks, and also that you'll set boundaries on their behaviour in a way that seems sensible and reasonable to them.

Early days of placement

We might reasonably think most adoptive dads are spared at least one inconvenience birth fathers must endure: sleepless nights. However, adopters of infants and older children report broken sleep – and often illness – in the early days of adoption. Being anxious is a great way of ensuring you don't sleep well, but it would be hard to imagine a relaxed adoptive parent in these first hours, days and weeks of parenthood. More importantly, the child may have a hard time settling, or may wake frequently in the night. Tired parents don't make fun parents or great decision-makers. Yet these night-time upsets present great opportunities for attachment. Foster carers may be guided by their agencies to avoid physically comforting distressed children in their beds, so as to avoid accusations of child abuse. This can mean children in adoptive placements have no experience of being helped to sleep after a nightmare, or even of being cuddled in their own beds.

Once the introductions are completed and the child has moved to the adoptive home, parents are often relieved to make the transition into their own regime, and make more of their own decisions. The standard works on adoption are good on the value of retaining foods, smells, textures and habits from the foster home into the new environment of the adoptive family home. For example, adopters are commonly advised to use the same laundry products as the foster carer, so the child's bedding continues to smell familiar. There is less advice available on how quickly adopters can begin to assert their own preferences, and to make changes in their child's environment. For example, a child may have been used to a fairly busy lifestyle in her foster home, and may have had to get along with a range of other children, including children who came and went from the foster family without explanation. Her new adoptive home may be designedly dull in comparison.

Should the adopters try to arrange a schedule of intense entertainment to make up for the reduced stimulus? Probably not. It is more likely the parents will want to create a calm and even soporific atmosphere, so the child is not unnecessarily over-stimulated. Coping with their change of circumstances is normally quite enough for even the most resilient child. Even quite young children clearly welcome the chance to relax in their new home. They may be happy enough spending the day exploring the new house and its immediate neighbourhood. And yelling throughout the night.

Adoptees often manage to relax faster than their adopters. Many adoptive fathers say the transition from "before" to "after" is sudden and alarming. Intense preparation, soul-searching and hoping is followed by the advice to relax. Prospective adopters are kept in a high state of arousal over a long period as they progress through the adoption process, and not all of them respond to placement with a release of tension.

Adoptive fathers make it clear that during their assessment, the social worker assigned to them would do her best – in a professional manner – to put the adopters off. Social workers are trained to look for the flaws that might indicate a poor prognosis for adoptive placement, and to help prospective adopters reject adoption if they are not suited to it. They do not "sell" adoption. It can therefore come as a shock when the placement starts, and the professionals working with the family suddenly begin to take the adopters seriously as parents.

Adopters can be wary of discussing issues of adjustment and attachment with their social worker during the placement, for fear of losing the children placed with them. Ideally, the relationship between the adopters and their worker will be strong enough to bear such discussions. However, there is no doubt that in the majority of placements the early development of feelings of love amongst the new family members can distort adopters' feelings about the role of their social worker. It would benefit many adoptive families to have access to counselling during this period, as a confidential alternative to discussions with their social worker. They could then discuss their emotional response without fearing their honesty will jeopardise the placement.

Typical traits of recently adopted children

All children are of course individuals, so any generalisations about their traits are likely to be somewhat trivial. Nevertheless, there is a small number of patterns in adopted children's behaviour that are common enough to stand out as distinctive.

It's rare for an adopted child not to demonstrate one or more forms of "delay". Immature speech is so common amongst adopted pre-schoolers that the non-speech-delayed youngster is a rarity. The traumas of their early life experiences, the disruption of moves and the uncertainty surrounding their young lives inevitably interrupts the development of children. Even the most resilient of children will experience some delay, simply by virtue of the emotional energy needed to deal with challenges children do not ordinarily face.

Pre-schoolers in care often have interesting speech that is not exactly faulty, and is often charming, but which can be labelled as delayed. Assessment by speech therapists will tend to reassure adoptive parents that the child's speaking ability is within range for her age group. But adopters commonly report that their pre-schoolers spoke immaturely and with poor grammar when they were first placed. This is usually a result of poor life experiences in the very earliest period of the child's life, when the basic neural pathways for speech are laid down in the brain. It's much easier to learn grammar when you're too young to understand how hard grammar is. Children who miss out on this learning phase must make up for it later on. It can be embarrassing for the adoptive parent if their child's speech is immature, since many non-adoptive parents will assume the child's speech is a sign of limited mental capacity. However, it's worth remembering that very few 18-year-olds say 'Me need car, daddy,' so your child's speech will come into line with everyone else's at some point.

School-age children present different patterns. Being of an age to better remember their lives with their birth families and foster carers, school-age children often carry a more obviously expressed reaction to their life's story. While younger children may act bizarrely in reaction to their early life experiences, it's usually hard to determine whether they're not just acting bizarrely because they are young children. School-age children are able to reflect on their experiences and draw conclusions from them – sometimes faulty conclusions – that can affect their moods and behaviours. As we learn more about the prevalence of depression amongst the child population, it should not surprise us if we find signs of depression in young adoptees. Loss, and our reactions to loss, can take many forms. Those frequently cited by adopters include lying, stealing and name-calling – those leading exemplars of "challenging behaviour". Prospective adopters are educated about these possible factors and their results.

Adoptive fathers seem to believe adopted children can be more persistent in "winding up" their parents than children in non-adoptive families. Adopted children may learn manipulative skills as a by-product of the coping strategies they develop in early life. The persistence of their behaviour is often regarded with a mixture of irritation and awe by adoptive fathers, with a sense of perverse pride in the children's stubbornness and creativity often coming to the fore. An ability to keep on at a parent, and to repeatedly test boundaries, is part and parcel of an adopted child's resilience. It can also be a positive indicator of their future independence and confidence.

Happy adopted children tend to "take liberties" at home even though their parents may not be temperamentally liberal. The fact that adoptive dads believe their children to be more naughty or manipulative than others may often simply reflect their lack of awareness of what is "normal" in any family.

Dads at home – temporarily

Adoptive fathers have been entitled to paternity leave since it was introduced in the UK in April 2003. Fathers have the right to two weeks' leave during the 56 days following the birth or placement of a child. One adoptive parent (if it is a couple adopting) can also claim adoption leave, a lower-paid parallel to maternity leave.

This new entitlement at least sets some kind of benchmark for paternal leave at the time of the placement, but it's based upon ensuring equality with birth parents rather than the special needs of the adoption situation. Many adoptive fathers say they did not have enough time with their children at the time of placement, though a few admit to being ready to return to work after a lengthy period at home.

Grief

For the Andy Capp stereotype of manhood, grief is what husbands get from wives when they show up late. Professionals who work with children have a different understanding of grief and its several stages. Based on the work of John Bowlby, who characterised grief as an essential adaptive response to loss, adoption workers recognise different manifestations of a child's reaction to loss depending on her age. Toddlers who are moved from their familiar carers will protest and may "search" for them. They may become preoccupied, keeping themselves busy, or become depressed and sleep a lot. They may also become emotionally distant and blank their carers. Older children show stages of grief that are more readily mapped to the grief reactions experienced by adults: shock, denial, anger, guilt, sadness or despair, and resolution. Children may need help in moving from one stage to another if they get "stuck", but it is important they be allowed to work through the stages, experiencing the emotions genuinely.

A child's grief is always distressing for her carer, but prospective adopters are prepared to expect grief and to support their child through its effects.

The period adoptive fathers take off work for the introductions period and start of the placement varies widely. At minimum, dads need to be available for the major part of the introductions period. Some men will be able to juggle reduced work commitments with the introductions, according to the flexibility of their work situation. However, men should be under no illusions as to the stress of this period, and even those who must continue with work at this time would do well to avoid scheduling anything too heroic. This is not the time to mount a hostile takeover on your firm's major competitor. For some men, it's hard enough to remember to shave and eat during this time, and the toughest can be brought to their knees by the sheer excitement of meeting their children and coping with the resulting emotions.

The early days of placement can also produce a surprising physical strain on adoptive parents. Lifting and chasing children can be a shock to the system if you're not used to it. Add missed hours of sleep and disrupted meal patterns and men can fall victim to stress-related illnesses.

Following the often physically gruelling and emotionally challenging nature of the introductions and initial placement, new adoptive dads say they have ambiguous feelings on returning to work. On the one hand, they miss the children; on the other hand, they are relieved to get back to "normality". It may be that every father feels this ambivalence, but adoptive fathers experience the duality in a very stark manner, and so may be more aware of it.

If they were not passionately and even tiresomely honest about their own feelings beforehand, the experience of the adoption process makes all adoptive fathers straight-talkers when it comes to their emotional life. It's one of the most attractive features of the average adoptive dad that he'll have all the good attributes of the new man without any of the suspicious baggage of guys who've chosen "sensitivity" as a lifestyle option by studying what women seem to like. Adoptive dads make good models for men who want to know what it's like to challenge the hard-exterior, soft-centre stereotype of manhood without opting for tree-hugging and a clunky new vocabulary.

What do adoptive fathers *do* in early placement? Adoptive dads say you need to be as involved as you can be. At this stage, no one really knows how family roles will shake out over time. But even if it turns out that the mother will do the majority of child care tasks, perhaps because the father is in full-time work, it helps if dad helps with all the tasks during the early part of the placement, during the time he has taken off work. Both parents will be able to share the experience of learning how to manage and care for the children, and discuss which strategies work and which don't.

Birth parents get to learn their children gradually, but adoptive parents are thrown into a crash course that has no syllabus or manual. Where a couple is adopting, two heads are definitely better than one. And where there are already children in the family prior to the placement, the involvement of the other children can help both practically and in terms of creating new family relationships.

Adoptive fathers usually do assume they will shoulder the traditional male roles in the family. This could be because adopters tend to be amongst the more conservative members of society, or because adoption preparation necessarily stresses the benefits of being an "ordinary family". Yet by taking on the organisational and logistical tasks within the family – not to mention the main earning role – adoptive fathers add to an emotional burden which some believe is not appreciated by people around them. Men go through emotional upheavals when they adopt, but do not always give themselves the time and space to deal with them. They also frequently try to juggle conflicting beliefs, causing extra stress.

For example, an adoptive dad may return to work soon after the beginning of the placement. The family will need the income he earns, his re-entry into work life will help him to relax, and the routine is good for the children. But at the same time he will miss the children, have had only a short time to get to know them, and won't be available to share the ups and downs of their adaptation to their new setting. While adoptive fathers, like many birth fathers, relish the return to work for the opportunities it affords for uninterrupted sleep, they also regret their reduced involvement in the family they are trying to build.

Mental reactions to placement

Many adoptive fathers experience a sense of "cognitive dissonance" as the initial excitement of the placement dies down but a sense of "normality" refuses to flood their lives. Cognitive dissonance is a term introduced by Leon Festinger in 1957. Festinger theorised that, when people feel a dischord between their behaviour and their beliefs, they will seek to remove the discrepancy:

> **[Cognitive dissonance] is the distressing mental state in which people feel they 'find themselves doing things that don't fit with what they know, or having opinions that do not fit with other opinions they hold'.**

People can avoid the distress of dissonance by changing their behaviour or their beliefs. For the adoptive father, the massive change in lifestyle introduced by the placement can lead to intense discomfort.

When pressed, adoptive fathers say they did not exactly feel a sense of unreality during the placement, but that they felt conflicting emotions in rapid succession. It's not unusual for an adoptive father to feel unrestrained joy in the company of his children, followed shortly by utter surprise that they are in his home. These emotions are at the opposite ends of an extreme, and each is experienced with a degree of self-consciousness. It's as though the adoptive dad is watching himself being happy, and watching himself being sad. As his world is subtly and not-so-subtly shaken up, it is not surprising that these mental effects occur. Old ways of thinking, being and relating are dissolving and new ones congealing. None of these breakages and bridges is built overnight. The reordering of the adoptive father's world takes time.

Are adoptive mothers immune to these feelings of confusion and ambivalence? My experience suggests mothers are as prone to these effects as fathers, but they generally have less opportunity to dwell on them. The majority of adoptive fathers map on to the mainstream of men everywhere: they leave the house each weekday morning and go to work. They live in two worlds, that of the home and that of work. Adoptive mothers who stay at home with their children have a more continuous and integrated experience of family life, and, some would say, less opportunity to agonise and theorise about it.

Nevertheless, all adoptive parents are in danger of experiencing some degree of depression if feelings of dissonance do not resolve themselves and instead develop into stressful preoccupations. Post-Adoption Depression Syndrome is recognised in the USA, but rarely honoured with a name in the UK. However, GPs recognise that the life changes associated with becoming an adoptive parent can trigger depression, especially in people with a history of depressive illness.

One popular means of predicting depression and other mental illnesses is the Holmes and Rahe checklist of stressful life factors. This scale gives a numerical rating for different types of life event, and asks you to total up your score. Death of a spouse is given the top value of 100 while moving house scores 20. Even Christmas will net you 12 stress points. If a candidate scores over 200, he is deemed to be at risk. Adopters can usually scoop up an armful of points from the test, and amass an even bigger score by adapting some of the labels to the adoption situation. For example, "Fight With Inlaws", assessed at 29 points, can be transferred to other adult members of the adoption circle including foster carers and, if only by proxy, birth parents.

Few adoptive fathers will need to take a test to acknowledge the depth and breadth of the changes adopting brings to their lives. But some may benefit from being reminded that the changes they are experiencing would have a profound effect on anyone. From the perspective of cognitive dissonance theory, they are in the process of changing their beliefs and/or behaviour in order to adjust to the world they find themselves in.

But should adoptive fathers experience dissonance at all? Haven't they been prepared for the life changes ahead, and shown they understand them?

First, actual experience is never the same as we imagine it is going to be. Classroom learning and extensive discussion can never fully prepare us for reality. What we learn can help us cope with challenges, but it cannot remove them for us.

Second, the focus on realistic expectations the prospective adopter is encouraged to have in regard to the child may not have been

Rusty mechanisms

Childless men avoid playgrounds, unless they want to get arrested. When you become an adoptive dad, you suddenly join the ranks of men who are allowed to go to playgrounds – who are expected to go to playgrounds. You never knew where they were before, but now you are intimately acquainted with the facilities of every site in town. For men who adopt children older than babies, immersion in the playground is the equivalent of the birth father's introduction to nappies and feeds.

And it's a strange experience. You find yourself wondering why no one has thought to lay on any latte. You'll also quickly identify a phenomenon from the non-adopter world, a man I call WD-40. This is the dad who is running around madly, chasing his kids with an energy that seems to betray more guilt than enjoyment. WD-40 is a spray lubricant that comes in a can, and that can unstick any lock, mechanism or bolt. But in my mind it stands for "Weekend Dad, Forty". He is one of the people you will meet who will remind you of everything you are not.

Adoptive dads are rarely comfortable with parenting in bursts. The commitment they build to their families during the adoption process and the first months and years of their child's placement ensures they will never see their kids as weekend diversions.

explicitly extended to his expectations of *himself*. He may have held on to an image of parental competence that evaporates in the heat of the placement itself. Or he may be so overwhelmed by the strength of his feelings that he forgets his carefully wrought coping plans. The strangeness of something we have longed for is one of life's most bittersweet surprises. Just as celebrities may turn out to crave privacy whilst loving (and being loved by) the camera, so adoptive fathers can find themselves simultaneously attracted and repelled by their sudden state of fatherhood.

The key word here is "sudden". Dissonance fades with time, as new experiences accumulate and become the new norm. Beliefs and behaviours adjust in response to the developing reality of the new family. This is unlikely to be a smooth or continuous process, and adoptive fathers may find themselves taking one step back to take two steps forward. It can be as hard for adoptive fathers to let go of some of their most elusive fantasies as it can be for their adopted child. Adoptive fathers need to mourn these losses too.

Successful placements

So, what *is* a successful placement? The adoption profession and its political masters naturally count those placements that do not break down or "disrupt" as successes. Prospective adopters need something more encouraging than this. According to social worker Sharon Walsh, a successful placement is measured over a lifetime. Her criteria are:

> **When a child grows up as a rounded individual and talks about being loved by their family. Where they are able to reach their potential because they were loved. And this is what we'd hope for *any* child, adopted or not.**

A new normality: Adoptive fathers and adoptive life

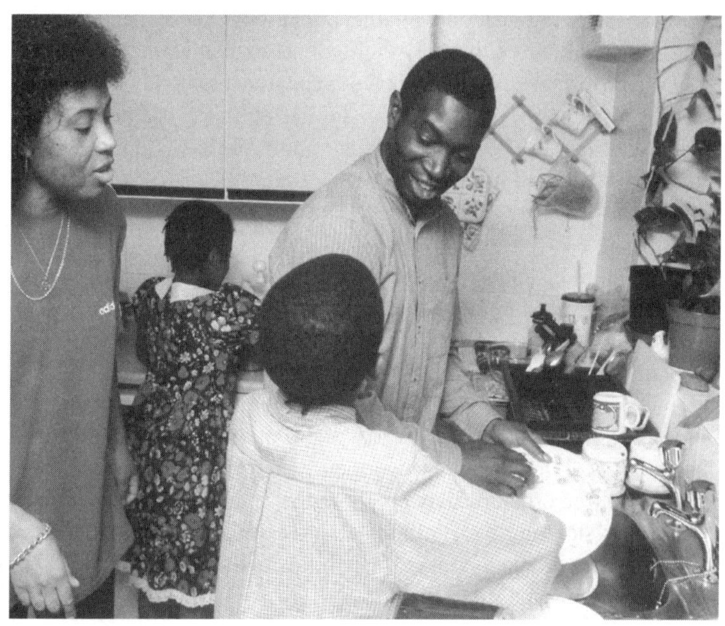

www.johnbirdsall.co.uk

Social workers call it post-adoption but we call it life.
Adoptive father

This chapter examines how novelty mutates into ordinary life for adopters, starting with the series of "firsts" that adoptive fathers find significant. We then look at how even as adoptive fathers settle to a new normality they retain their awareness of the special nature of their role as a Present Father. We see how their awareness of the facts and mechanics of adoption can inhibit adoptive fathers.

We then look at how adoptive fathers deal with their expectations of their children, and particularly their educational attainments. We see how adoptive fathers find their own authenticity as fathers during the process of parenting, how adoptive fathers cope with parenting challenges, and the adoptive dad's common role as the custodian of his child's recorded history.

First things first

At what point is "placement" replaced by "normal family life"? From the technical point of view, the granting of an adoption order signals a successful placement and the beginning of the legally-recognised new family unit. However, although the moment of legal adoption is an important symbolic rite of passage for most adoptive families, it does not confer any magical properties on the family. They may feel they have reached their equilibrium long before the granting of the order, or may continue for years after the order with the feeling that their family life is an interesting, and unpredictable, experiment. And it is possible for families to experience both feelings at the same time.

Yet adoptive fathers say the achievement of a series of "firsts" helps them mark the family's progression to normalcy, if only in the eyes of the professional team around them. The first exchange of contact letters is often seen as an important milestone, as is the child's first birthday in the adoptive home, and the first anniversary of her arrival. One adoptive father cited this chain of "firsts" as the tool used by the family's agency to delay decision-making on whether their adopted child's sibling would be matched with them. From the adopter's point of view, more precious "firsts" with his son took precedence, such as the moment his son first stared into his eyes.

The first tantrum and the first snore are equally surprising, and both may make it to the adoptive dad's inerasable mental scrapbook. Parents of all kinds treasure their children's "firsts", but adoptive parents do not have the default response of wondering if any particular behaviour represents a trait inherited from themselves. Indeed, they are more likely to look for a negative association with the child's pre-placement background or genetic heritage. Experienced adoptive dads report that both responses are usually wrong: children are individuals, and what they do is as surprising as what anyone does. Their early rituals, obsessions and amusements mutate and fade as they grow, so too much concentration on whether a particular event has roots in a gene or an early life experience is usually a waste of time.

The first "ordinary" days are usually those that adoptive families savour the most. What would, to established families, seem like a rather boring day can seem wonderfully "right" to the recent adoptive family. Walking the dog, sweeping leaves, slumping in front of a video: these are the unglamorous, but authentic, activities families share, and the times during which they find their own rhythms. For adopters, a long period of preparation can make the experience of "normal" family life blissful.

Adoptive fathers never lose the sense that they are somehow special: that they have been given a special opportunity in life, and a special relationship to which they owe a lifetime's commitment. But this is not to say adoptive dads feel like great people all day long, every day. Like everyone, they experience the trivial as well as the sublime. And they experience particular moments of ambiguity that do not trouble birth parents. One way to describe this ambiguity is the occasional, paradoxical feeling an adoptive father may have about childlessness. He may feel like a childless person – with children.

This strange dual reality can kick in without warning. It sometimes happens when another dad talks about a time in his own child's life that corresponds to a period in the adoptive dad's life when he did not know his child. The adoptive dad and the adoptee have missed out on some potential experience together here, and the reminder usually comes as a shock.

Another trigger for this strange feeling can be differences in parenting style. A birth dad may breezily recommend disciplinary strategies that an adoptive dad would never dream of applying, or he may imply that the adoptive dad spoils his children. The adoptive dad may well have got over crippling self-consciousness in the early days of the placement, but exchanges like these can trigger old feelings of inadequacy or oddness.

Furthermore, these feelings can strike entirely at random. Adoptive dads report looking sometimes at the children they know and love so dearly and wondering who they are, and what they are doing in the house. These aren't deep, existential thoughts about origins and attachments, but sudden moments of strangeness, perhaps of alienation. It could be that most adoptive dads never fully reconcile themselves to their role in life. But before we get too alarmed at this prospect, it's worth remembering most people never get quite used to the way they look in photographs or the way they sound on tape. There's always a slight glitch between our mental models of ourselves and the personal feedback we receive from the world, and perhaps our children act unwittingly to draw attention to these mismatches. If so, then the sudden, fleeting feeling of strangeness could be the flipside to the birth parent's occasional, random sighting of a relative's mannerisms in the behaviour of a child. All parents are sometimes jolted by their children's demonstration of their otherness. Adoptive dads may guiltily ascribe these feelings to the adoptive relationship, whereas birth dads experience similar effects and ignore them.

This self-consciousness applies at a very practical level for all adoptive dads, though it is naturally more acute in some than in others. Adoptive dads are likely to feel they are under scrutiny. The oddness of the earliest days of the placement becomes magnified in public, when the feeling of being in the spotlight can quickly distort an adoptive father's self-assessment of his abilities. And, being on

A reality check for the self-critical

Since the danger of self-consciousness is ever-present in the early months (or years, or decades), it's worth asking for a reality-check whenever you feel you're being singled out for criticism as an adoptive father. Some general observations may help here:

- **All shop assistants assume that any man in sole charge of an infant is a hopeless fool who should be watched carefully and given gratuitous advice (such as the classic 'She's just in front of you'). The invisible sign around your neck spells "Uh oh – dad", not "adoptive dad".**
- **None of the dads in your child's class can remember the names of the other children's mums and dads either. That's what the women do.**
- **It is a very rare dad who finds the company of small children so engrossing that he craves it 24 hours a day. Every single parent on the face of the earth needs occasional respite from their children – and their children appreciate the break too.**

People do indeed make instant judgements about others, and parenting seems to be a no-holds-barred arena where some folks just can't help affixing labels and proffering unsolicited advice. You may feel that you are being unfairly targeted for more than your share of this traffic, just because of your adoptive status. But it's far more likely that if you are indeed suffering a high rate of interference or comment, it's because of the signals you're giving, not the legal status of your family. If you feel uncertain about your ability to parent, then that's entirely normal. If you feel uncomfortable with your uncertainty, that's when the protective or corrective instincts of other people will kick in. As you become more comfortable with how *you* function as a parent, and how *your* family works, you'll attract less of this kind of attention. Another way to say this is: *relax*. But telling me to relax has only ever resulted in my getting more annoyed, so I wouldn't dream of saying it to you.

the whole performance-obsessed beings, this can rapidly erode some men's self-esteem.

For better, for worse

Is the life of an adoptive family any different to that of any other family? One social worker told me cannily:

> **There *is* a difference, but I wouldn't tell them what it is, because they have to figure it out for themselves.**

It's hard to escape qualitative judgements in any area of life, and adoption is no exception. Is it "better" to be adopted or "worse"? Are adoptive parents "braver" than other parents? While these questions are understandable, they are unanswerable, and, after you have lived with them for a while, essentially meaningless. No one can judge the quality of an individual's life on an absolute scale. Relative judgements only work when there are suitable alternatives to judge against. But in the case of adoption, the alternatives are always speculative. Would an adopted person's life have been happier with her birth parents, or with another adoptive family? There is no way of telling. The best we can say is that in the judgement of the people responsible for the child's future at the time of placement, adoption seemed the best path for the child.

Every adoptive father I have spoken to has said that being an adoptive parent is neither "better" nor "worse" than being any other kind of parent – but that it is different. At the same time, most adoptive dads manage to stress that being an adoptive father is the same as being any other kind of father. It seems the "difference" adoption brings to a family swims in and out of focus, depending on the nature of the situation.

For example, an adoptive family may have to avoid visiting a particular locality in order to avoid potential meetings with members of the child's birth family. With some children being adopted away from their birth locales for safety reasons, this is a common restriction amongst adoptive families. As the child grows up and becomes less easily identifiable, the risk may lessen. However, for as long as the risk remains, the family will have its "difference" triggered by the mention of a particular town, or seeing its name on a signpost.

As adoptive fathers gain in confidence during the early years of a successful placement, they seem able to draw clear boundaries between their new lives and the lives they left behind. Couples who were childless tend to look back on their "years of freedom" with a mixture of affection and mellowed sorrow. They may remember the stresses of fertility treatment but appreciate the time and money they had at their sole disposal. This is no different from the situation of any parent, though the adoptive father may have a sharper appreciation of the dividing line between the old life and the new one, and the energy the family expended on breaking through it. Many men talked of "life being turned upside down" when the children arrived. For adoptive families, the launch of their life together is unavoidably a cataclysm of some sort. It's not something that can be drifted into.

The early days of placement point up another area where adoptive parenthood is different rather than "better" or "worse". Adoptive parents need support during their first days, weeks and months with their children. But so do birth parents. It's not the amount of support that differs, but the type of support. For example, a parent of a new baby may need reassuring she is holding and feeding her baby correctly. The adoptive parent of an older child may need to be told it's quite usual for quite old children to revert to immature behaviours when they are placed with their new parents; they may, for example, completely forget how to go to the toilet. This phase passes in time, and can be seen as a positive sign of attachment: the child feels secure enough with the new parents to replay some of her earliest experiences, and perhaps symbolically enact her growing trust.

Advice of this kind is only likely to come from someone familiar with adoption, which is where the support network developed during the preparation period shows its strength. Other kinds of support can come from friends, family and neighbours who happily don't know one end of a Form F from the other. New adoptive parents often need short periods of time apart from the children to check in with each other without distraction. Birth parents can think this is amusing, since they may not have had such luxuries themselves. But adoptive parents can explain that, having spent so long planning and discussing the placement with each other, it makes sense for them to assess its progress with the same level of diligence. And anyway, everyone can do with a cup of coffee and a piece of cake every now and then.

Perhaps surprisingly, little of a family's adoption preparation time is devoted to the rewards of adoption. Most preparation programmes do indeed pay attention to the upside of adoption, and may include sessions aimed at the positive effects for all members of the adoption circle. However, in the wider context of a complete adoption preparation and assessment period, much more attention is given to what can go wrong in adoption.

As a consequence, adoptive parents can sometimes be oversensitive to potential problems with their children and react to crises that are not really present. The danger of "problematising" ordinary situations may be more likely of the man in a couple, since he is less likely to be the primary caregiver. While adoptive mum is busy nurturing their child, adoptive dad may be seeing imaginary signs of attachment disorder in every dropped toy or refusal to eat, sit, stand, put a coat on . . .

Adoptive fathers who take the role of primary carer seem to meet the same problems of male carers of all kinds. One told me that other fathers say they envy his lifestyle, 'then their eyes glaze over'. He believes most fathers see their role solely as entertainer and enjoyer of "the nice bits" like bedtime. For these dads, "quality time" means high-quality time for *themselves*, not necessarily for the children. The same adoptive father said it is hard for a male carer to be accepted in parent-toddler groups, and described the "three-chair exclusion zone" he encountered the first time he attended such a group.

Adoption as an issue

A child's adoptive status can act as a magnet for free-floating anxieties about family life and the parent's role in it. For example, a child may be having regular tantrums long after the point when "the books" say she should be over them. Does this mean she is reacting to the fact of adoption? Is she somehow reliving early life experiences? Or is she expressing anger at the losses in her life?

It's more likely "the books" are wrong. Any child care book has to generalise, and health professionals will quickly tell you that practically every attribute of a child can be measured on a very large spectrum. Einstein didn't speak until he was three (and incidentally went on to give up his first child for adoption). And many children continue to throw regular tantrums, even after they have been appointed as CEO of a major company. Is your child being stroppy because she was adopted or because she *is* stroppy? In the end, it doesn't matter. You – and she – still have to deal with the situation as it is. Tracing the origins of her behaviour may be enlightening to you both, but such a trace is unlikely to resolve the situation in itself. You still need to do the work on changing her behaviour to something more acceptable to the family and more rewarding for herself. It's time to solve problems, not contemplate their sources.

Parents may feel that ignoring the adoption factor is a denial of the family's roots and reality. If the fact of adoption were suppressed and its mention punished, then this would clearly be an unhealthy situation. But this does not mean adoption is an appropriate focus for concern in every situation.

There is an analogy with non-adoptive families. A family with a tantrum-centric four-year-old may speculate about the child's genetic makeup. But this speculation won't help them move forward. Dragging out the family tree every time there's a challenge in the family will quickly become tedious – and a trigger for pointless arguing.

Newish adoptive dads tend to identify the rewards of fatherhood with their fresh status as "normal families", doing whatever normal families do, whether it be arguing in a car park or ordering a Happy Meal. More seasoned adoptive dads tend to point to the developments of their children, and their delight in seeing them settle down, make friends and enjoy themselves.

Expectations and projections

Adoptive fathers often report a lack of set expectations about their child's development, talents or achievements. This may sound harshly disinterested, as if adoptive fathers cannot summon up any genuine involvement in the lives of their children. In fact, the reverse is true. A lack of expectations is not the same as having low expectations. The distinction between birth fathers and adoptive fathers is that it is generally easier for an adoptive dad to suspend any instinctive prejudices he may have about the way his children "turn out". For most adoptive fathers, this very lack of expectations is a source of excitement and joy. It means they are more likely to be surprised by their children, and more likely to be appreciative of their unique personalities as those personalities emerge. Adoptive fathers are not looking for some particular set of behaviours to emerge and confirm or destroy their dreams for their children. They are instead engaged with the child on life's great journey: the discovery of our individuality. One adoptive dad stressed that his role involves setting a good example wherever he can, but otherwise watching to see his children's talents emerge.

This approach can be especially important for children who have behavioural or developmental problems. While other parents might be agonising about their six-year-old's inability to complete *The Times* crossword, an adoptive dad might be pleased at the extra time available to kick a ball around, or to blow soap bubbles. This is not to label adoptive children as poor achievers, but to recognise something parents of all kinds would do well to remember: the formal accomplishments we recognise in school are not the only measure of a person's worth. Nor are they necessarily a large component of any child's happiness.

Schools vary in their recognition of the effects of adoption on children. The attitude of any school will be highly influenced by its intake. Schools with a wide mix of social backgrounds and abilities will tend to downplay the significance of adoption. While some adoptive fathers see this as a denial of their children's special needs, others recognise that an unblinkered attitude to the varying needs of children of all kinds can be beneficial for the treatment of their children.

Adoptive fathers tend to have a positive approach to problem-solving when it comes to educational matters. Although fathers of all kinds try to take a greater interest in their children's progress at school than earlier generations might have done, adoptive dads are geared towards taking constructive action to support their children's development. By not having pre-fixed ideas about a child's ability – a situation which usually amounts to an imagined height to which we expect the child to climb – it is easier to focus on the child's real attainment and ask what kind of help she might need. Adoptive dads often welcome statementing – the process whereby a child's extra educational needs are formally assessed and a plan put in place to provide them within the school setting. For other parents, and especially well-educated, middle-class parents, a statement for their child might seem like a terrible, and terribly public, failure. Adoptive parents are spared these unnecessary blushes. They know their children's formal educational needs are important, but that they form one part of an array of factors that combine in their development. Adoptive dads tend to be aware their job is to enable their children to grow up, and to grow up to be themselves. This responsibility requires them to see every resource that may help their child as a boon rather than a form of value-judgement.

Adoptive fathers welcome progress in their children, being generally achievement-oriented and on the look-out for signs they are making a difference to their child's life. The progress they note is usually radically different from the casual boasts made by parents at playgroup or school, and they are unlikely to share breakthrough moments with people they do not know well. For example, one adoptive father said how pleased he was that his son could now watch *The Tweenies* for as long as 20 minutes at a stretch. This isn't going to mean much to the non-adoptive dad who has already found subtle signs that Junior is going to need a better Reception Class teacher if he's to make it to Cambridge or Harvard on time.

As well as being keen to distinguish their own needs for status and reassurance from their children's own needs, adoptive dads tend to cheerfully accept professional help from outside the family rather than regarding external intervention as a mark of shame. Many adoptive dads recount their battles to find and fund the right kind of psychological assistance for their children, and tell of the great advances made by their children when the right resources are found. Their struggle to acquire appropriate help is sometimes made in response to the requirements of the agency and despite the same agency's lack of practical help. But adoptive parents are at least spared the heart-searching and sometimes avoidant behaviour of non-adoptive parents whose children need help with some aspect of behaviour, cognition or learning. Adoptive parents are carefully prepared to expect their children will have special needs, and that they will have to work to understand those needs, become expert in the available therapies and programmes, and fight to get them.

And, to a man, every adoptive father I spoke with said his child's situation was nowhere near as bad as the worst scenario he could have imagined. This may be an unromantic approach to child development, but their clarity and preparedness for action gives adoptive parents an advantage over non-adoptive families, where childhood problems may be undetected, denied or laid at the door of the child's teachers.

I also believe from my discussions with adoptive fathers that they relish the chance to fight for their children's needs. Some adoptive dads would not be happy without a battle to be fought on behalf of their children. Explicitly acknowledged or not, the chance to fight on behalf of someone who otherwise has no voice and champion is a key motivator for adoptive dads. When talking about their children's needs they talk about "fighting for the help she needs" and "hammering on doors", and always, always "*pushing*". Perhaps a preoccupation with pushing is the active component of the Present Father, and we should think of his *presence* as also incorporating *pressure*.

The adoptive relationship can help parents avoid the unnecessary guilt that sometimes attends children's attainment or lack of it. As one adoptive father told me, 'You don't have limiting expectations, so it's more clear that life's a great adventure.'

Finding the father within

> **How can I grow to care if all I want is my**
> **old life back?**
> **How can I grow into being a father?**
> **When will I be good at this?**[1]

This adoptive father's anguish is plain in the urgency of his questions. Self-consciously present adoptive fathers can believe family life presents a new series of tests and trials, more bewildering and hurtful than those of the pre-placement phases. They tend to set themselves high standards, and to feel guilty at mourning the loss of their previous lives.

Successful adoptive fathers do grow into their roles, but there is no template or schedule that can guide them as to what to expect of themselves, or when they will begin to feel competent and at ease. Adoptive fathers can become frozen in a cycle of self-doubt and self-criticism. Those who have a tendency to perfectionism and limited support networks are the most vulnerable.

[1] From a poem by an adoptive father, *Adoption Today*, August 2003

Many adoptive fathers deal with their early discomfort by pursuing practical family projects. For example, fathers frequently cite their determination to have "proper holidays" as soon as they can. This may mean seeking approval from the local authority to get a passport for a child in placement who has not yet been legally adopted. Asking for the necessary clearance gives the social services department a chance to express any views it may have about the advisability of taking the child abroad so soon after she has joined the new family. The textbooks seem to suggest that any movement outside the new family home will bring great stress to a child in placement, who may not be certain in her own mind that she has arrived at her "forever family". Yet there can be no guidance on when it will be safe to travel without such feelings intruding. Is it a month, a year, three years? For children who have experienced the loss of their birth families, there may never be a "safe" time. Every departure, every change, may spark memories of that first separation. But for other children, and for most children at most times of their lives, movements of this kind will not be an issue. Adopted children tend to be resilient, often much more so than their non-adopted peers. The people best placed to make a judgement on such issues are their parents. Adoptive parents can therefore find themselves asserting the primacy of their own judgement quite early on in a placement. And they must be able to back up their judgement with a plan for how they will cope if their judgement turns out to be faulty. This is, in a sense, what they will be doing as parents for the rest of their lives. It might as well start sooner than later.

Adoptive dads in particular can feel very strongly about family holidays. If the father is the sole earner in the family, then holiday time is the only opportunity he has for extended time with his children. The chronic shortage of family "face time" affects all fathers, but adoptive fathers are likely to feel its effects more acutely. They may feel their family relationships need more nurturing than those in birth families. Sadly, it's probably more true that *all* types of families need to work at their relationships, and need more time in which to do so.

The determining factor in such situations is the passion of the parents. Where they strongly believe travel will help the family to enjoy itself, and present useful experiences for the children, their belief in its value will outweigh any potential risks to the children's sense of stability.

This example highlights a core element of the transition from prospective to actual adoptive family: the replacement of generic models with specific ones. Or, if you prefer, the removal of vague, generalised ideas about what is good for adoptive families in favour of strong, particular plans based on the needs and preferences of the children themselves. This is an important breakthrough for any adoptive family. It's the point where the advice of social workers, the material from preparation classes, and the books (even this one) are shunted into the background and the parents' judgement takes over. The parents won't make all the right decisions; but they must begin making their *own* decisions, and learning from the way events unfold.

Adoptive fathers often play an important role in this transition because they are quite likely to have one or more strong beliefs about their family life that they are determined to pursue. It may be they think the children need to play sport once a week, or that the family should go out to eat together regularly. Whatever their particular focus, adoptive fathers often have a family agenda for life outside the home.

Bringing their own agendas to the family situation and making those agendas work with the needs and preferences of the children is a major part of the adoptive parents' family-building activity. There are inevitably compromises, but compromise is itself an important part of family life. One adoptive father said that, although his life revolves around his children, he doesn't let the children stop him doing what he wants in life. It seems then the reality of family life is a group of people somehow revolving around each other in a complicated, but hopefully graceful, dance.

Families change over time and rarely have the opportunity or inclination to review their own progress. Relaxed adoptive fathers tend to take a long-term view of their role and its effects, opting to reserve judgment on their own performance. One told me:

> **It's a long-term investment – we won't know for twenty years if we've made a difference, but at least we're giving them the chances in life they wouldn't otherwise have had.**

Natural born fathers

Men disarmed by fatherhood

Adoptive dads often seem to have absorbed the resigned judgements of their female peers. One told me 'I think men have an awesome capacity to be pathetic.' It may be that all men suspect man is the weaker sex, but most of them avoid voicing their suspicions. Due to their artificially heightened sense of their responsibility as parents, adoptive fathers may be more open to articulating this suspicion than other dads. The assessment process, and the emotional trials of the entire adoption journey, may give some adoptive fathers a taste for personal disclosure that makes them appear more insightful than other men who are not given the same opportunities to get in touch with their feelings.

It is noticeable that birth fathers often describe the intensity of their feelings at the birth of their children, and almost seem to allocate all their feelings about parenthood to this one event, while adoptive fathers tend to describe their emotional reaction to fatherhood as an extended process full of change and confusion. Perhaps as a society we use the birth father's presence in the delivery room as a way of approving and managing men's emotional involvement in parenthood. If so, the adoptive father's more elongated experience – a slowed-down and patchily edited miracle – is perhaps a richer rite of passage and one more in line with the complex transition to motherhood.

Most commentators take the view that fatherhood is socially constructed. By this they mean that fatherhood is defined by society depending on the beliefs and values operating at the time. This theory quickly generates figures such as the Victorian patriarch, supposedly distant from his family and mostly concerned with covering the bare legs of pianos, and the post-war, pipe-sucking corporate dad, playing catch with Junior at the weekend. But as we know, the images of fathers presented in the media do not necessarily coincide with the reality as lived by millions of men. Adoptive fathers, as men who self-consciously take on a parental role in the full glare of professional scrutiny, may find these received images more stressful than birth fathers, and may put more energy into their emulation *or* rejection of them than fathers who are less anxious about their role.

This approach to understanding fatherhood naturally tends to describe the father's role in terms of what is left over after the mother's role has been assigned. Some commentators are beginning to offer an alternative view, whereby fathers bring a distinctive and universal quality to the role of parenting. In other words, the very fact of being a man contains the code for a particular set of fathering actions and styles: 'fathers do *other* things, not *mother* things'.[2] In one version of this theory, men have the potential to be fathers buried in their genetic makeup, but their ability to parent is only triggered by the presence of a child. Other theorists – so-called generativists – believe that fathering is universally encoded in men but does not require a releasing trigger. Loosely speaking, generativity is the idea that men come to decide, during their own development, to invest in or take care of other people. Men's motivation in changing their world views so fundamentally is somewhat obscure in this theory, and the "trigger" model of generativity as a coping response to the changes

[2] Burdon, Barry (1998) *Generativity in the early years of fatherhood*, paper presented at *Changing families, challenging futures: 6th Australian Institute of Family Studies Conference*, Melbourne 25–27 November 1998; http://www.aifs.gov.au/institute/afrc6papers/burdon.html. Dr Burdon is here quoting from MacKey, Wade C. (1996) *The American Father: Biocultural and Developmental Aspects*, Plenum.

imposed on their lives by fatherhood seems more reasonable. The "universal" generativity approach seems to claim a creative spirit for men, viewing every man as a more or less conscious author, a begetter of someone who will outlive him and somehow carry on his spirit.

Certainly adoptive fathers are obliged to articulate their motivations for fathering. To descend rudely from the heights of ethnology, adoption workers' overriding interests in a prospective adopter's motivations centre around his propensity to abuse children in his care. A prospective adoptive dad might take comfort in the "trigger" model of fatherhood, believing the act of becoming responsible for a child will release his latent talents as a father. He may envy birth fathers who will not have been questioned on their motivations in conceiving a child, and who (he trusts) evolved overnight into competent, caring fathers – their male heritage rising, as it were, to the occasion. But a social worker will have a much less romantic concept of triggering and the behaviours environmental changes can unlock. A man cannot be a child abuser without access to a child.

In this light, the "universal" model of willed, creative fatherhood is more useful to adoptive fathers. Believing that the desire to care for others is a natural part of his growth will help him to rationalise his feelings about adopting someone else's child. But I cannot help suspecting this theory of fatherhood is just as culturally determined as the earlier stereotypes we now deride. It adds a heroic spin to the messy reality of most men's lives. Adoptive fathers act in a complex and shifting mix of habit, instinct, intention, theory, misunderstanding, hope and belief – just as any other parents do. The difference between adoptive fathers and non-adoptive fathers is likely to be the degree of introspection and judgement they bring to their own fathering behaviour. They know their children have already suffered loss and abuse, and they are rightly concerned not to add to their children's deficits, but – where possible – to compensate for or reverse those setbacks. Their lives are projects. They cannot watch their family lives develop from the standpoint of interested observers. They know they count.

The practical effect of these factors can create discomfort and distress for some adoptive fathers. One told me:

> **I work long hours so my wife is with the children more. If I have suggestions [about parenting] she'll have more reasoned and researched reasons for her opinions and I have to defer to her. She's with them more and she can see through the surface of problems . . . So sometimes I feel I'm here to bring in the money and provide a male role model. If that sounds slightly childish, then it is. But she keeps the kids to herself, so it's a case of me joining them.**

Other adoptive fathers find their role unexpectedly wider than the one they were expecting. As a Bristol University study of non-infant adoption outcomes discovered:

> **Adoptive fathers thought it had been assumed that they would take a minor supportive role. They provided important emotional support for their partners and took over more of the parenting tasks. Many fathers were far more involved in parenting than they had been with their own children and most enjoyed this role. Other men found they had to provide the "mothering" as well as "fathering", as children refused to allow adoptive mothers to care for them. Some children refused to be put to bed or eat food prepared by adoptive mothers. Far more attention needs to be paid to the role of fathers in assessment and plans for support.**

Doubts and divergences

Most adoptive fathers admit to moments of doubt about their decision to parent. These do not seem to be reasoned revisions of their original thinking but fleeting reactions to challenges in the family. They therefore tend to express their moments of doubt in terms of positive responses to negative events or feelings. In other words, they offer advice on how to keep going during the bad times.

One experienced adoptive father gave two pieces of advice, both of which take the form of instructions to the self. The first is to remember you are "good enough". It's easy for adoptive parents to be overtaken by perfectionism. Their struggle to become parents and the challenges of dealing with adoption issues within the family give them a keen awareness of their responsibilities: an awareness that can become exaggerated. When family life doesn't go smoothly, it never helps if one or both of the parents are distracted by feelings of failure or guilt. Adoptive dads are perhaps more prone to these feelings than non-adoptive dads, who may have responded to the challenges of parenthood in a less self-conscious way, and without the scrutiny of professionals.

The second piece of advice is complementary, and even more robust. It is to "remember they won't be with you forever". By recalling that our time with our children is, on the timescale of human life, relatively brief, current difficulties can be put in perspective. A child's current challenging behaviour will not last forever. The adoptive family is supported by two opposing forces: chance and intention. Remembering you are "good enough" recognises the chance element of all life stories, and honours the fact that families can only do their best, and no more. Remembering childhood is short recognises that adoptive parents choose their path in life, and must remake their commitment if they feel it faltering. These nostrums may be simple to state, but they are profound in their effect. They are both designed to restore perspective in times of stress, and to reconfirm the journey the family is taking together.

The divergence of ideals and practice is not peculiar to adoptive fatherhood. All parents, indeed all people, find at some time or another they are not fulfilling their dreams. When we are fair to ourselves, we recognise how unlikely it would be for anyone to live exactly according to their intentions. Real life gets in the way. However, the weight of material, process and emotion generated by the adoption process can divert an adoptive father's attention from this truth. His child's "case" may take up an entire cupboard; and the child's discovery and arrival in his life may have carved months out of his schedule. He has stood up in court and promised to care for the child. There are expectations on his shoulders.

It takes time for men to wear these expectations lightly. Where the primary carer is a woman in a male–female partnership, a sensitive adoptive dad may silently take on an imagined duty to the community while his partner gets on with the more practical matters of raising the child. The adoption preparation phase necessarily encourages introspection, and examination of the emotional life. Men may not be able to switch off this habit of thought, may be unused to exploring such issues, and uncertain how to recover from the emotions they induce. The complex emotions they experience as they meet and get acquainted with their children keep the cauldron bubbling. Many men are deeply confused by their sudden mission of love. Can they fall in love with this child? What is love? It is it anything like "attachment", which the social workers talk about? Few men can remember when they last had a meaningful conversation on the topic of love. Yet adoptive dads take on love as a project. The bizarreness of this mission can never be fully erased by preparation. Unsurprisingly, men sometimes take refuge in adoption-related tasks that either contain only a small emotional element (such as paperwork) or tasks that allow them to vent their feelings on people outside the family.

Some adoptive fathers felt they had not been adequately prepared for what one called "dealing with the aftermath of your own feelings". For example, adopters may be taught "holding strategies" for dealing with tantrums. The rage expressed by adopted children can be awesome, and when a child is quite strong it may fall to the father to do the holding. An out-of-control child is more frightened than her parent, but also better able to move on once the episode has past. Adults are left in a state of heightened arousal, often questioning whether they have taken the right action, and wondering if they are the source of the child's anger. Men are not generally well prepared to deal with their own troubling emotions, and even an adopter who was a healthcare worker with experience of emotionally charged situations said he had difficulties with challenging emotions in the family environment.

Although adoptive fathers learn to be open with their feelings and gain some facility in talking about their own styles of interaction, motivations and so on, they still tend to be guarded on one topic women find easier to discuss. This is the effect of the adoption process on their relationship with their partner. Adoptive fathers are unlikely to talk about the strain imposed on their relationship by the adoption journey. Although every adoptive father uses the word "rollercoaster" to describe the emotional component of the journey, few explicitly cite problems in their relationship as a part of that wild ride. Yet, talking to adoptive *mothers*, it's clear that the adoption process does challenge couples – and it would be surprising if it didn't.

Women are, of course, adept at getting together and discussing the uselessness of men. My sense is that women regard men as the weaker vessel when it comes to containing and transporting the emotions. The intimate, rigorous and protracted nature of preparation and assessment, and usually of the matching phase as well, gives men ample opportunity to show their wobbliness. I was fortunate to talk largely to people who had recovered from any difficulties with their partner relationships, but there is no doubt that the normal tendency for couples to break or drift apart – the background radiation of marriage, if you like – is exacerbated by adoption. Couples who thought childlessness tested them to the limit may find new subterranean layers of disappointment and despair in their adoption journey.

To make another bold, and probably foolish generalisation, it may be that while men find it less easy to discuss and understand their feelings, women often do not appreciate the genuineness of their menfolk's concentration on probabilities and strategies. Men really do see parenthood as one of an infinite set of roles they might play. Parenthood rarely has any emotional precedence over any other alternative role. In order to match their partner's investment in and prioritisation of motherhood, men recruit all kinds of thinking strategies that may strike women as bizarre or irrelevant. A religious conviction, for example, may be much more important to the man than the woman.

Custodian of memory

It often falls to the adoptive father to act as the guardian of his child's documentary records. These records include the mass of forms completed about the child, and her life story book: an account of her entire life, compiled in a way she can follow and understand. These documents need safeguarding and updating. Men may take on this task because it will otherwise become buried beneath the more urgent needs of daily life.

Adoptive fathers may therefore find themselves frequently initiating conversations with their children about their history. All adopters are encouraged to communicate information in a way that is "age-appropriate". In other words, adopted children have a right to know about and be helped to understand their own life stories, but need to be protected from material or interpretations which they will not be able to absorb or which may mislead or frighten them. The usual stages of child development mean children can only take certain concepts on board at certain points in their intellectual growth. So, for example, while a child of eight or nine may suddenly be ready to understand what it means for her to have lost her birth parents, she will not be capable of understanding the legal nature of adoption and therefore its security. Equally, while a younger child may be able to repeat the basics of her life story, giving the name of her "tummy mummy", listing her foster placements and concluding with her move to her "forever mummy and daddy", this recitation will not have the full force of meaning for her that it will later acquire. It is, however, valuable for her to know and repeat this history, because she will have some understanding it is special information about herself, and also because it ensures the main facts of her life form a familiar pattern that carries forward into later stages of comprehension.

Adoptive parents are usually given professional advice about the vocabulary they use to discuss adoption issues with their children, but like all advice this does not necessarily stick, and when it does it can easily become unglued in the heat of everyday family life. Adopters are encouraged to say "birth mother" or "tummy mummy" and avoid using "natural mother", but some adoptive fathers find such usages clumsy and reason that as long as they don't imply any disapproval or other negative attitudes while conversing with their children about their early lives then their interactions will be safe and useful. Referring to "biological dad" may summon up irrelevant images of soap powder. Language is also subject to shifts as once-sanctioned terms lose their power or come to be questioned for their utility. The phrase "forever mummy and daddy" is probably the only romantically-tinged phrase endorsed by social workers, but even this is now no longer actively encouraged. Adoption workers accept that not all adoptive placements work out, and that therefore making a promise about "forever" can be harmful.

There is no detectable common difference in the way adoptive fathers discuss their children's history as compared to adoptive mothers. However, men may be more inclined to pursue gaps in the child's history in order to complete her life's picture. Holes in the child's history act as entry points for fantasy, and as apparent evidence she was not important enough to be noticed. Adoptive parents' failure to close such gaps can compound the insult.

Adoptive fathers may take on the role of prime patcher of the facts in the child's life story, partly because this is something dads *can* do when their partners are the prime carers – and possibly because men enjoy the sense of vicarious indignation they can feel on behalf of the child for the sloppy treatment of her history. As a result, adopted children often end up with better documented and better understood life stories than children in non-adoptive families. Children in non-adoptive families pick up the family lore by osmosis, but they may also thereby pick up false impressions. This shouldn't be of concern in most families, but adoptive families need to do all they can to build and buttress a sense of unique and valid personality in a child lacking the benefits of a dull, conventional start in life.

One significant difference adoptive fathers note in their family lives in comparison with non-adoptive fathers is indeed the theme of life story work in adoptive families. A child's life story is usually developed during the time the child is in care, at the stage when adoption is decided as a path for her future. The child's social worker, with help from the foster carer, collects details about the child's life to date, including the places she has lived and the people who have been significant in her life. Wherever possible, photographs and dates are included to make the document as accurate as possible. Although in her early years the technical accuracy of her life story book will not be of much concern to the child, in later life the degree of care taken with the content of the book can be immensely valuable in helping her with her developing sense of self. Life story books allow adopted children to own and manage a concrete, personalised record of their lives, giving firm identities to their birth families and foster families, and anchoring their growing understanding of themselves in real facts. It is well known that adopted children can develop fantasies about their origins. In fact, all children fantasise about their "true" identities, commonly dreaming they were adopted! But for adopted children, clarity about their origins, and respect for those origins, are important factors in their emotional development and ability to make safe and rewarding relationships.

Adoptive parents therefore find themselves talking with their children about topics other families might regard as intruding on the special innocence of childhood. Conversation about the child's early life experiences must be carried out in an age-appropriate way, otherwise the child will be confused and possibly alarmed. Children's ability to understand their own stories modifies with time. Similarly, adoptive fathers report that discussion of their children's life stories is best when initiated by the children themselves, although many also mention they sometimes raise the topic if there's a "hook" in the immediate environment, like a mention of adoption or childbirth on a TV programme. Discussing adoption openly with the child from as early as possible is the best way of avoiding "bombshell" days, which so many adopted people of older generations experienced. It is unthinkable that an adopted child today would not know she was adopted. However, adoptive parents can, by avoiding the topic, cast a taboo around the subject that becomes harder to break the longer it is left in place. Adoptive children as young as three can relate their life story in terms of a sequence of their "tummy mummy", their foster carers and arrival with the adoptive parents, even though understanding of the functions and relationships involved is many years away. But familiarity with her own story from an early age gives an adopted child a foundation upon which she can build gradually as her understanding of the world and her relationships with it grows. The role of adoption in creating her family then emerges alongside her growing understanding of herself, other people, and how people get along together.

For adoptive fathers who are labouring to understand their new family in the early days of placement, echoes from their child's early life provide an additional seasoning. While pre-school children may have been subject to appalling trauma in their early lives, it is rare for their experience to translate simply and cleanly to some noticeable form of behaviour. Many adoptive fathers say they found their children surprisingly "normal", given the training they were given about the effects of grief on children and their knowledge of what their children suffered. But they will often move on to describe surprising behaviours or habits their children exhibited, and to report nightmares and night terrors. The connections between experience and behaviour are complex, and always easier to see in retrospect, or with the help of a good therapist. It's harder to spot a connection between early experience and current behaviour when the current behaviour is dripping down the wall and congealing on the carpet while its producer stares at you with a mixture of hostility and curiosity. At times of stress, theory can be hard to apply. Adoptive dads, who on the whole spend less time with their children than their partners do, may be apt to forget the special circumstances in their children's lives and overreact to provocations. All children test their adult carers, and adopted children have more reason to test, and to re-test. If you have been let down by adults in the past, and possibly denied your most basic needs, you're not going to take new adults on trust, even if they have a nice smile and the best intentions.

Where adoptive fathers intuit that issues from the past are causing difficult behaviours in their children, they often place their focus on providing alternative models. The provision of strong role models and behavioural examples was probably the strongest common theme amongst the men I spoke to when writing this book. Perhaps modelling is what our culture expects of fathers: they may not be able consistently to meet the basic needs of a child, but they can demonstrate the traditional virtues. As a society, we look to fathers to embody virtue, or moral excellence – and castigate them when they fail to do so. The word *virtue* has its roots in the concept of the attributes of men (Latin *vir*).

Adoptive fathers' preoccupation with setting positive examples is, I believe, an aspect of Present Father Syndrome. It is also related to the male need for action: they believe doing something – anything – is better than doing nothing. Men in our society are not traditionally good at experiencing life in a detached manner, preferring to see themselves as actors. This has a distinct benefit: men are propelled to take action on behalf of their children, especially when dealing with external authorities such as social services departments, schools and health professionals. Some adoptive fathers clearly relish the chance to do battle with the authorities, and many do so with impressive efficiency, employing all the techniques of assertiveness and organisation they may use to equally good effect in their work lives. We sail close to gender stereotypes here, but it's hard not to see the adoptive dad acting out the protective warrior role on behalf of the "weaker" wife and child. But much of this battling behaviour is sanctioned by professional practice in adoption, which stresses the importance of advocacy for the child, protection of her rights, and due care for her personal history.

Adoption support

Continuity in social work care for adopters is not all it should be. Many adoptive fathers reported a distinct lack of support from their social workers as the placement progressed, with some remarking that the social worker's responsibility ends with the arrangement of a placement. I think most social workers would agree their goal is not placement but *successful* placement, and that their duties to the adoptive family therefore extend well beyond the early days of placement. The new adoption legislation in England and Wales makes an assessment of adoption support requirements mandatory.

Several adoptive fathers mentioned that their local authorities seemed to have been by-passed by the customer care movement. Some were angered they were given little respect by social workers with whom they dealt, and treated as potential trouble-makers by other staff. Respect for adopters is enshrined in the new standards for adoption currently being rolled out in England. But this kind of mandated respect will not help the adoptive dad who calls into a council office and is treated by reception staff in the same way as a claimant of housing benefits. He is unlikely to demand special treatment as an adoptive parent – and more likely to wonder why claimants of housing benefits need to be treated brusquely in the first place. Middle-class and privately employed adopter clients of local authorities are often shocked by their first exposure to their local authority premises and its atmosphere.

In general I found post-adoption support was felt to be lacking in families who had adopted through local authorities. This situation was not confined to families where the adoption had occurred some years previously, when post-adoption support was less well recognised as a factor in successful placements. It may be that constraints on resources and attention to targets result in lowered attention for post-adoption activities in some local authorities. Families who had used the leading independent adoption agencies were offered more extensive post-adoption facilities, including courses and workshops.

Lack of formal support from "the professionals" was, I suspect, regarded with ambivalence. On the one hand, adoptive dads may feel let down by promises of support that did not materialise, and protest the denial of resources to their child. On the other hand, they may delight in the absence of "interference" from the agency. Many adoptive fathers stress the importance of finding their own support networks, seeking specialist help where needed, and developing their own judgement. They universally say the practical help and advice they need comes from friends and other adoptive parents. Where they judge they need professional help, they tend to go directly to therapeutic specialists rather than to social workers.

Setting out to love someone

Mainstream media features on adoption frequently used to be headlined with variations on the title of the Beatles' 1967 hit *All You Need Is Love*. Adoption specialists have countered with their own taglines that seek to redirect readers towards a more realistic understanding of adoption, culminating with the phrase used as a title for the BBC's documentary about five adoptive families screened in 2000: *Love Is Not Enough.*

Adoptive fathers seem generally saddened that their loving

motivations to become parents are suppressed during the adoption process. Every adoptive father I spoke to loved his child, and every dad said they could not now imagine life without the child who so randomly joined her life with his. But none gave their love of children as a motivation for adopting. A love of children is discounted by social workers as something that is either too vague to analyse or too common to dissect.

The truth is that love is irrelevant in the assessment process. The applicant's capacity to care for, nurture and respond to the needs of children is very much at the centre of the assessor's concerns, but whether these abilities can or should be wrapped in the term "love" is neither here nor there. Many adoptive placements succeed without the family members ever managing to demonstrate the kind of "love" that would pass a Hollywood slush detector. Social workers are not trying to build a romance, but to ensure a secure and happy future for children who have been denied safety, stability, encouragement and peace in their early lives. They are working with children who are often severely emotionally damaged – children whose best espousal of love may be to steal from their adoptive homes, or to hold eye contact with an adoptive parent for one isolated moment every passing day.

Adoptive fathers tend to be eloquent on the subject of love, perhaps because it's an ever-present mystery in their lives. They will acknowledge the challenges their children present, and the exasperation and despair that is sometimes engendered when things are going badly. But they cling to an underlying, and even unjustifiable, love for their children.

> **The Bible says children are a blessing and a gift and I'd go with that. But it doesn't say the gift has to come from you. It doesn't matter "whose" they are.**
> Adoptive father

Supporting adoptive fathers: What and who can help

www.iStockphoto.com

I wasn't prepared for how painful the process was going to be. You can't communicate how painful it is. You can't tell anyone . . . [My son] couldn't be more wonderful.
Adoptive father

In this final chapter we draw together adoptive fathers' insights into the adoption process and how it affected them. The aim is to help those who work with prospective adoptive fathers, and their friends and families, to support them through the adoption journey.

This chapter also gathers together the advice adoptive fathers offer to those men thinking about adopting. The adoptive fathers I spoke to emphatically endorsed the rewards of adopting but were under no illusions as to its challenges. They were all concerned to share the actions and attitudes that had helped them build their families.

Emotional roles

Adoptive fathers generally reported high levels of stress during the adoption process, with the sense of importance attached to these feelings declining roughly in line with the passage of time since placement. But even relatively "cool" adoptive dads of several years' standing remembered specific frustrations or insults that could still ignite their anger or derision. Most adoptive fathers said their relationships with their partners had, if anything, improved as a result of the stresses of the process. 'We share the ups and downs, the hugs and cries', said one, referring again to adoption's famous emotional rollercoaster. 'You get the whole spectrum of emotions', he continued, 'even in the course of one day.'

The shared trauma of the assessment, preparation and matching periods is borne more or less equally by adoptive partners, which perhaps gives them certain advantages over couples where the woman is pregnant and the man is relegated to the role of uncomplaining supporter. Couples are, however, seemingly likely to share their emotions so that while one is "down", the other is "up". This was reported so commonly that it may be a candidate rule for adoptive couples: expect your own emotions to be the opposite of your partner's, and to switch emotional positions with them frequently.

However, our emotions rarely synch exactly with another's, so adoptive dads may exaggerate the polarised nature of the positions partners take. Adoptive fathers may also fall more readily for the role of "enthusiast", and so attempt to outweigh any signs of depression by their partners with unnaturally jolly or optimistic behaviour. All of us have a sneaking regard for cheerful slacks-and-slippers dad, cheering the family on with light-hearted and lightweight assurances that "everything will be fine", and adoptive fathers may on occasion be more susceptible to playing this role than other dads.

Support networks

Those who work with prospective adopters would do well to encourage and even seed the construction and maintenance of family support networks. Adoptive fathers are clear on their need for support, and their interest in supporting their peers. They are not always clear whether their need for support derives from their adoptive status or their fatherhood status. But no adoptive father pronounced himself satisfied with the breadth or depth of his network.

The adoption process exposes the private lives of prospective adopters to intense scrutiny. One result of this process is that few approved adopters easily retreat to an entirely private, self-sufficient life. Adoptive families tend to be aware of the permeability of the family boundary, and recognise the potential contributions of friends, family, school and healthcare professionals. They are open to help.

However, society is not geared to the efficient creation of father networks. Men meet each other through work and play, but not usually through parenting activities. Even when men collide in playgrounds and schoolyards, they tend to find it difficult to strike up acquaintanceship with each other. Adoptive fathers in couples often rely on their partners to acquire father-friends for them through their own networks.

Agencies can help here merely by encouraging prospective adoptive fathers to talk to each other and stay in touch. They may also provide workshops for fathers as a means of maintaining the network. They can also let prospective adopters know that joining an organisation such as Adoption UK is an ideal early step, and one which will bring them into contact with other adoptive dads.

Counselling

The adoption process exposes and sometimes also causes deep pain amongst adoptive fathers. Few I spoke to had been offered counselling to help manage their developing feelings. Some adoption professionals regard the potential attachment problems of adoptive families as so serious that family therapy should be offered as a right at the start of every placement. Others argue this is unnecessarily dramatic. And I suspect all British social services departments would agree that the funding does not exist to provide such a blanket service.

Nevertheless, I believe the potential for acute anxiety and depression amongst adopters is real enough to be of concern to adoption workers. While social workers may stress that adopters should take care of themselves and find ways of managing the stress of the process, adopters can be understandably reluctant to admit to feelings of despair or helplessness. Prospective adopters do not want to fail their assessment; adopters with placements do not want their children taken away. Those who work with adopters can make a very simple and powerful contribution by encouraging adopters to own their feelings, however difficult or frightening those feelings may be, and to seek help from their GP.

A proactive approach to the emotional and cognitive well-being of prospective adopters can have a profoundly positive effect on placement success rates. At least one local authority agency has a pre-adoption specialist whose role it is to "save" prospective adopters who might otherwise not pass their assessment. These specialists meet with prospective adopters who are having difficulties with their home studies and prepare special sessions, materials or referrals to help them work through whatever issues they have. Obviously, not all prospective adopters will be approved, but it is to be hoped the majority who make it through their home study and pass their security checks can, with help, become successful adoptive parents. It makes good business sense to intervene as early as possible to ensure a successful outcome.

Contact and reunions

Adoptive fathers differ little from adoptive mothers in their attitudes towards contact and reunions with their children's birth family. One US study found that 'in general, adoptive fathers were less involved than mothers in this process [of managing contact with the birth family] across time'. There's an expectation men will be more hostile than women to the idea of an initial meeting with the birth parents, on the assumption an adoptive father will feel he is competing with the birth parents. I did not find anything to suggest this is true. Every adoptive father I spoke to who had met his child's birth parents stressed it had not been something he relished doing, but had been extremely valuable.

Letterbox contact appears to be an issue managed equally by adoptive parents in terms of planning and attitude, though it may be that in couples the woman makes most of the practical effort. My own experience is that it's hard for birth parents and adoptive parents alike to find much of significance to say in letters; the fact the letters are being exchanged, and kept, is their true value. As children become older they are able to contribute more to letterbox contact if they wish. It's also possible for them to communicate by phone and email, and alter the terms of their contact arrangements to include renewed face-to-face contact. Changes in adopted children's feelings about their birth families change as the children change, and adoptive parents are aware of this.

The widespread use of the internet has complicated the business of reunions. Adopted people are encouraged to use the services of an adoption agency to help them reconnect with their birth families, rather than track them down and turn up unannounced. The majority of adult adoptees searching for their birth families were adopted under different circumstances than pertain today in the UK. They have every reason to hope a reunion will be a welcome or at least viable option. Given the mobility of the population, the internet would seem an ideal way of matching up birth family members who have lost each other.

However, children adopted today mostly come from difficult family backgrounds, usually involving abuse. Birth families using the net to advertise for their children may be exposing them to danger. Adopted children who do not comprehend the full details of their early background may not see why they can't respond to an appeal from their birth family. Adoptive parents need to alert their children to the "stranger danger" of the net, and also work with them to understand how those close in terms of blood may need to be kept at a safe distance. Contact and reunion without openness and support can threaten the stability of families – adoptive and birth families alike.

What adoptive fathers want of social workers

Many adoptive fathers mention the importance of having a good social worker, especially during the matching period. The comment is often made in the context of friends' experiences with social workers who were unavailable, unhelpful or unfriendly. Of course, expectations and perceptions vary, so it is impossible to say whether "good" and "bad" social workers exist. However, it is clear what most adoptive dads mean by a "good" social worker. They mean:

- one who takes them seriously, listening to their concerns and answering their questions;
- one who pursues potential matches on their behalf;
- one who keeps them up to date on progress.

This is a fairly small set of requirements, and it centres around the social worker's role as an information channel. The matching period can often be one of apparent inaction as matches are pursued, forms exchanged and meetings arranged. Contacts between agencies happen at a normal business pace, which may nevertheless appear glacial to the adoptive parent.

As in most endeavours in life, the more competent people you have on your team, the less stressful the project. Adoptive fathers are usually comfortable with approaching the adoption process in this light. It fits well with the practices they are likely to use in their work lives. It also helps to reduce the sense of isolation that can otherwise overwhelm adopters, especially during a protracted matching period.

Men also want their social workers to be more upbeat. Many experienced adoptive fathers gave the opinion that the social workers they met over-stressed the difficulties of adoption, and paid little attention to the rewards. I may have been fortunate in talking to adoptive fathers who have (or believe they have) "easy" children, and have missed fathers of more challenging children. It may also be true that adoptive fathers normalise their own family situation, so that, over time, whatever pertains in their family is seen by them as reasonable since they are, after all, coping with it. Women may suspect that fathers who are too cheery and dismissive about difficulties within their families are simply not paying attention, or exercising a little denial. Whatever the reality of their family situations, most adoptive fathers seem to believe the outcome is much more rewarding than that advertised by their professional colleagues.

The facts, in most cases, may be simpler. Social workers are obliged to communicate all the possible outcomes in an adoptive placement. They must not leave any prospective adopter in doubt about what *could* go wrong. Placements can and do break down. Some children do not thrive in adoptive placements, or reject them. Some adopted children are challenged by behavioural or emotional problems that no amount of love and direction can alleviate, and sometimes the ending of the placement is the only way forward for all parties. Adopters must understand all these possibilities before they submit themselves to formal approval as adopters.

The majority of adoptive placements are, as far as we can judge, successful. It is therefore inevitable that most adoptive fathers are spared the worst extremes of the possible outcomes they explored during adoption preparation. They may suspect their social worker of being unnecessarily pessimistic, and, especially as the years roll by, wonder what all the fuss was about. I imagine the only quarrel an adoption worker would have with this assessment is the "un-" prefix in "unnecessarily pessimistic".

If social workers are champions of the child's interests, and expressly not concerned with "selling" adoption to prospective adopters or encouraging adopters' loving instincts, should adopters find their own champion? Someone who will encourage them, reassure them and fight for their health, happiness and security? The best social workers seem to morph seamlessly into such angels as the placement progresses. However, continuity of this kind is not always possible or practical. Even where such continuity exists, adopters do well to retain and recruit for their network. They need a large, and continually growing, network of supporters, sitters and soundboards.

Adoptive fathers can become so involved with the adoption process that they begin to regard themselves as experts in the field, and become critical of social workers who fail to live up to their expectations. For example, they may distrust social workers who appear confident, optimistic and "bright and breezy" about the placement of a child in her care. The discrepancy between attitudes demonstrated by the adopter's social workers and the child's is often remarked upon by adoptive dads, with many feeling they are better versed in the realities of adoption than some of the children's social workers they meet.

They can also be critical of the foster homes where their children have been cared for, typically mentioning that the children received inadequate stimulation or individual attention. Some adopters also have to confront situations where the foster family wanted to adopt the child in question, but were not approved as adopters, or approved but not matched with this child. This is a difficult situation for all concerned, and one where a focus on the needs of the child helps to control everyone's emotions and behaviour. I have a sense that the men respond to the competitive nature of this situation, and their response can combine both triumph and anger – at actions which they perceive as being disruptive or undermining on the part of the foster carers. Women tend to empathise more readily with the pain and disappointment of the foster carers, who must not only deal with their loss but also manage the onward journey of the child they wanted to keep.

Some men can become hypersensitive at this stage in their lives, with every sloppy statement on the part of a social worker or friend taking on grand proportions. As a notorious deep-ender myself, I sympathise with the outrage of the adoptive father whose social worker cut through his discussions of the child's challenging behaviour with the statement: 'You're lucky because you got a blue-eyed, blonde girl.' Crude stereotyping often seems designed to pull well-meaning adoptive parents away from their mission to understand their children, recognise their needs, and meet them. Perhaps even the most professional social worker can tire of theory and be tempted to jolt her clients into action. But again, if this is so, the difference with the preparation and assessment phase is marked.

Distilled advice from adoptive fathers

Adoptive fathers are remarkably unanimous in the advice they offer to other men thinking about adopting. I have summarised their advice in this section.

Ask lots of questions of anyone and everyone you can find

You will discount many of the answers you get, but you need to hear yourself asking. You need the widest range of experience and opinion you can get so that you can cherry-pick what seems helpful to you as you negotiate your adoption journey and construct your own fatherhood role. The more questions you ask, the more empowered you will be and the less lonely you will feel.

If you don't think you'll be able to cope, then don't do it

. . . But remember that few birth dads are 100 per cent confident about their ability to be parents. You need to be confident enough in your abilities to be good enough. If you become an adoptive father, you won't exactly be a national hero. If you decide adopting is not for you, you will not be a national disgrace.

Build a support network, and keep extending it

Adoptive fathers need strong and diverse teams to help them parent. Be ruthless in your recruitment of people who can help you. Pay them back in ways they value.

Prepare for the worst, but hope for the best

It may be a cliché, but this advice combines the two key aspects of the motivation to adopt in a useful form. Adopters need to be practical but must also have a vision. Neither attribute is enough in itself. It's not enough to have an excess of love: you must also be willing to hold a screaming child night after night. But if all you have is supreme competence, and no empathy with the emotional needs of a child, then you will surely fail as a parent. The trick is to keep preparing, to keep renewing your hopes – and to celebrate the progress your child makes on her journey through life.

Look after your relationship with your partner

If you have a partner, this relationship is the foundation of your family. Children change families, and adopters should not assume they can switch to a new, busy family life without continuing to invest in their own relationship. Couples need to remember and celebrate their love for each other, so their self-esteem does not wilt under the barrage of new demands made upon them by their children.

Be aware of adoption's role in the family, but try not to use it as a label

Adoption does present special circumstances, but it is not always the source of or solution to challenges that crop up within the family. Adoptive fathers need to be aware of the issues of identity and attachment that accompany adoption, and must confront the potential effects of their children's early life experiences. But they must not let the family's adoptive status intrude where it has no relevant part to play.

Make time for your family

Work – even the work of writing about adoptive fathers – can be a convenient excuse for avoiding your children. Fathers exploit their work commitments as a way of avoiding family life more often than they care to admit. It may be a less dysfunctional escape route than alcohol, drugs or infidelity, but overwork can contribute massively to family problems. The greatest gift you can give your children is your time.

The next greatest gift is to teach them how to make their own time. Too many children are hoisted aboard a crammed timetable of activities that sucks up every waking minute and trains them for a life of unquestioned busy-ness. But children who have been in care, even for a short period, have tasted all the stress they need for a good many years. When they arrive in an adoptive family, they get the chance to *be*. You may find yourself "wasting" an hour while your toddler examines every stick and stone between your house and the playground, but she will learn more on that trip than she will being whisked to the park in your car. And you will both have tasted the true meaning of quality time: time that is beyond value, because it is time together.

> **One of the first words [my son] said was "happy".**
> Adoptive father

Afterword: What adopted children learn from their adoptive fathers

Sheena Macrae wrote these words on adoptive fathers' impact on their children's lives for a Father's Day article entitled *A Dash of Dads*.

> **Our children can learn from their fathers about loss, pain and joy in forming an adoptive family. A man who is open to speaking of his feelings about how he formed his family tells that men as well as women can affirm feelings, can speak of joy when the adopted family grew as the child and the parents learned how to be attuned.**
>
> **It's not just learning that Dad was on board when the adoption happened: a father speaking of his thoughts and family aspirations allows adopted children of both genders to open up the landscape of inner fears and hopes.**

This fatherly engagement with feelings is what an ability to talk with kids engenders. It is particularly important during the stresses of our children's teens. Sure kids may laugh (fathers need thick skins) but they are listening, and they will talk (if not to us, to their friends). Maps for that landscape of inner fears are much more easily found when their need is acknowledged. If fathers can talk about their losses, are seen with active conscience around concerns (such as racism) that impinge on the kids and have actively promoted both strength in the family (routes forward) and roots (connection to the birth family) then kids are going to see their adoptive father as having delivered them relatively safely towards adulthood.

References

Avery R (1997) 'Adoptive parents are overwhelmingly in favour of opening sealed adoption records, Cornell study finds'; http://www.news.cornell.edu/releases/Jan97/adoptionrecord.ssl.html

Berry M (date unknown) *Risks and Benefits of Open Adoption*; http://www.futureofchildren.org/information2826/information_show.htm?doc_id=77505

Bettelheim B (1987) *A Good Enough Parent: The guide to bringing up your child,* London: Thames and Hudson

Birkett D 'The Oracle of the Ovary', *The Guardian*, 19 August 2000; http://www.guardian.co.uk/weekend/story/0,3605,355818,00.html

Brodzinsky D, Marshall S and Henig R M (1993) *Adoption: The lifelong search for self*, New York: AnchorBooks; as discussed by Rita Blockman, Doris Houston and Phyllis Picklesimer (undated) 'Presenting a positive view of adoption', *Connections Newsletter*, National Network for Child Care [USA]; http://www.canr.uconn.edu/ces/child/newsarticles/FCS513.html

Burgess A (1997) *Fatherhood Reclaimed: The making of the modern father*, London: Vermilion

Costs and Outcomes of Non-Infant Adoptions, [undated], Hadley Centre for Adoption and Foster Care Studies, University of Bristol School for Policy Studies; http://www.bris.ac.uk/sps/downloads/Hadley/costs.pdf

Cousins J (2003) 'Are we missing the match? Rethinking adopter assessment and child profiling', *Adoption & Fostering*, 27:4

Dad: the magazine for new fathers, Issue 1, Spring/Summer 2003, published by FathersDirect

"Daniel", 'Preparing for adoptive fatherhood', *Adoption Today*, Adoption UK, Number 95, November 2000

Department of Health (2001) www.doh.gov.uk/adoption/standards.htm

Equal Opportunities Commission (2003) *Fathers: balancing work and family*; http://www.eoc.org.uk/EOCeng/EOCcs/Research/fathers%20 balancing%20work%20and%20family%20(english).pdf

Festinger L (1957) *A Theory of Cognitive Dissonance*, Palo Alto: Stanford University Press

Finley G E (1999a) 'Children of adoptive families', in Wendy K Silverman and Thomas H Ollendick (eds) *Developmental Issues in the Clinical Treatment of Children*, Boston: Allyn and Bacon, p 358

Finley G E (1999b) 'Unheard voices: adoptive fathers on the adoption process and adoptive fatherhood', International Conference on Adoption Research, Minneapolis

Hill D (2003) 'Being there is not enough', *The Guardian*, 15 January 2003

Howarth P (ed) (1997) *Fatherhood: An anthology of new writing*, London: Victor Gollancz

Real Magazine, issue of 25 March to 4 April 2003

Lord J (2002) *Adopting a Child*, 6th edition, London: BAAF

Office of National Statistics, *Adoption Orders: Social trends 33*, January 2003; http://www.statistics.gov.uk/StatBase/ssdataset.asp?vlnk=6381& Pos=2&ColRank=1&Rank=160

Stuttaford T 'Mad? No, but loves change', *The Times*, 24 July 2003

Useful organisations

British Association for Adoption and Fostering (BAAF)
Head Office
Skyline House
200 Union Street
London SE1 0LX
Tel: 020 7593 2000
www.baaf.org.uk

Be My Parent
Skyline House
200 Union Street
London SE1 0LX
Tel: 020 7593 2060/1/2

BAAF Cymru
7 Cleeve House
Lambourne Crescent
Cardiff
CF14 5GP
Tel: 02920 761155

BAAF Scotland
40 Shadwick Place
Edinburgh
EH2 4RT
Tel: 0131 220 4749

Telephone Head Office for details of other regional and country offices.

BAAF is the leading UK-wide organisation for all those working in the adoption, fostering and childcare fields. BAAF's work includes giving advice and information to members of the public; publishing a wide range of books, training packs and leaflets as well as a quarterly journal; providing training and consultancy services to social workers and other professionals; and giving evidence to government committees on subjects concerning children and families.

BAAF also publishes *Be My Parent*, a monthly newspaper that features children needing permanent new families. You can send off for a free information pack to the address above.

Adoption UK
46 The Green
South Bar Street
Banbury
Oxfordshire
OX16 9AB
Tel: 01295 752240
www.adoptionuk.org

Adoption UK is a parent-to-parent network of over 3,500 established and prospective adoptive families. It welcomes enquiries from prospective adopters; offers local support groups all over the UK; and publishes a wide range of useful leaflets and *Adoption Today*, a bi-monthly magazine written by and for adopters, which also features children waiting for adoption.

The Association for Families who have Adopted from Abroad (AFAA)
Carlton Lodge
Woodhead Wortley
Sheffield
S35 7DA
www.afaa.org.uk

A network of families who have adopted from abroad and offer support and advice to others considering the same.

Useful resources

Jenifer Lord, *Adopting a Child*, BAAF, 2002 (6th edition)
BAAF's best-selling guide describes what adoption means and how to go about it. It tells you about the kinds of children who need new families, what sort of people agencies are looking for, and the legal aspects and costs of adoption in the UK or from overseas. It includes a list of agencies around the UK that you can approach for more information.

Amy Neil Salter, *The Adopter's Handbook*, BAAF, 2004 (2nd edition)
This guide sets out clear, accurate and precise information about adoption before, during and after the big event, to help adopters help themselves throughout the adoption process and beyond. Topics covered include education, health, adoption support and legal issues. Contains a useful resource list of organisations that parents can approach for more information about a wide variety of topics.

David Howe, *Adopters on Adoption*, BAAF, 1996
In this absorbing collection of personal stories, adoptive parents whose children are now young adults describe the importance and distinctiveness of adoptive parenting.

Be My Parent
A UK-wide monthly newspaper for adopters and permanent foster carers who may or may not be approved. It contains features on adoption and fostering and profiles of children across the UK who need new permanent families.

For a free information pack and subscription details, contact 020 7593 2060/1/2

Adoption Today

Adoption Today is a bi-monthly journal published by Adoption UK and is available on subscription. It keeps members in touch with one another, profiles children needing new permanent families, and gives information on general developments in the field of adoption.